The
QUOTABLE
KENNEDYS

Other Collections by Bill Adler

THE KENNEDY WIT
THE COSBY WIT

The QUOTABLE KENNEDYS

EDITED BY BILL ADLER

AVON BOOKS ◆ NEW YORK

AVON BOOKS
A division of
The Hearst Corporation
1350 Avenue of the Americas
New York, New York 10019

Copyright © 1997 by Bill Adler Books, Inc.
Interior design by Kellan Peck
Published by arrangement with Bill Adler Books, Inc.
Visit our website at **http://AvonBooks.com**
ISBN: 0-380-79328-8

Library of Congress Cataloging in Publication Data:

  The quotable Kennedys / edited by Bill Adler.

    p.   cm.
    Includes bibliographical references
    1. Kennedy family—Quotations. 2. United States—Politics and government—
1945–1989—Quotations, maxims, etc. 3. United States—Politics and government—
1989—Quotations, maxims, etc. 4. United States—Social conditions—1945- —Quotations, maxims, etc. 5. United States—Foreign relations—1945–1989—Quotations, maxims, etc. 6. United States—Foreign relations—1989- —Quotations, maxims, etc. I.
Adler, Bill.
CT274.K46Q86   1997   96-53680
973.922—dc21   CIP

First Avon Books Trade Printing: June 1997

AVON TRADEMARK REG. U.S. PAT. OFF. AND IN OTHER COUNTRIES, MARCA REGISTRADA, HECHO
EN U.S.A.

Printed in the U.S.A.

OPM   10 9 8 7 6 5 4 3 2 1

Contents

Introduction

It seems that America will never get over the Kennedys, and thus the Kennedys will forever have something to offer America.

In 1994 Patrick J. Kennedy was elected to the U.S. Congress by the first district of Rhode Island, where he joined his father, Teddy, and his cousin, Joseph II. We have not had a Kennedy triumvirate in the federal government since Teddy was first elected to the Senate in 1962, while Jack was president and Bobby was attorney general. Teddy, Patrick, and Joe may soon be joined by Kathleen, the first Kennedy woman to make a serious entry into politics. Although her first run for Congress was thwarted, she now is in public service as lieutenant governor of Maryland. Meanwhile, John Jr. tests the waters through his magazine, *George,* an insider's guide to politics.

But we cannot expect a replay of the 1960s. The first thing that any Kennedy seems to realize is that each new generation must reinvent their views, and reestablish their role as Kennedys. Their founding father understood this, and encouraged independent thought and political growth. The only thing we can be sure of is that politics runs in their blood, and our lives, and our children's lives, will be touched by one or more of the rapidly expanding Kennedy clan in years to come.

The
QUOTABLE
KENNEDYS

· 1 ·

The Kennedy

Family

Being a Kennedy

This is the most exclusive club in the world.

> —*Joseph P. Kennedy. Remark*
> *while admiring his children,*
> *in-laws, and grandchildren at*
> *a family get-together.*

The Kennedys are a self-contained unit.

> —*Rose Kennedy. Interview,*
> *early 1930s.*

The strength of the family is our greatest national treasure.

> —*Edward M. Kennedy. Speech,*
> *May 26, 1976.*

[Dinner conversation was] mostly monologues by my father . . . well, not exactly monologues. But we didn't have opinions in those days. Later, the discussions included us more, but mostly about personalities, not debates on political issues and things. I never had any particular interest in political subjects in those days.

> —*John F. Kennedy. Remarks on*
> *family talks while he was a*
> *teen.*

After the West Virginia primary in 1960, a contest Kennedy was supposed to have lost, Charles Spaulding witnessed the mutual admiration between John F. Kennedy and his father. As Jack was approaching, the elder Kennedy remarked:

Just look at him. How does he do it? I couldn't have done it. Not a chance.

> —*Joseph P. Kennedy.*

When Joseph left momentarily, it became John's turn to admire:

It's amazing. People knock the hell out of him every time they get a chance. They forget that he has accomplished as much in his lifetime as three or four men.

> —*John F. Kennedy.*

Jacqueline Bouvier Kennedy adjusted to the Kennedy family gradually:

The Kennedys are terribly bourgeois.

> —*Jacqueline Bouvier. Remark soon after her engagement to John F. Kennedy, 1953.*

How can I explain these people? They were like carbonated water, and other families might by flat. They'd be talking about so many things with so much enthusiasm. Or they'd be playing games. At dinner or in the living room, anywhere, everybody would be talking about something. They had so much interest in life—it was so stimulating. And so gay and so open and accepting.

> —*Jacqueline Bouvier. Remarks after first meeting the Kennedys in Hyannis Port, Cape Cod, 1953.*

Just watching them wore me out.

> —*Jacqueline Bouvier. Remark on the Kennedys' level of activity, 1953.*

The only word the Kennedys know is "terrific."

> —*Robert F. Kennedy. Quoted in* Life, *November 18, 1966.*

There are cherished memories here. Some may bring a tear to the eye. . . . The last thirteen years have passed so quickly. So many things are different now. Yet the value of these words remains—to keep us going when times are rough; to remind us of what he meant to us as son and a brother, a husband and father; to carry us back to those great days when his energy, spirit, and brilliance came together in that glorious adventure we shall never realize and never forget.

> —*Edward M. Kennedy. Introduction to* Words Jack Loved, *a collection of tales about John Kennedy's love of reading presented to the family for Christmas 1976.*

It is from the family that we gain the strength, the hope, the aspirations, the guidance, and the support to be effective and productive members of society. It is from the family that we learn to produce wholesome and viable communities where individual talent and creative initiative can enjoy the fullest expression

> —*Edward M. Kennedy. Speech, September 11, 1976.*

It means that we're just exactly the same as everybody else, except better.

> —*David Kennedy, son of Robert F. Kennedy. Response to the question "What does it mean to be a Kennedy?"*

I can get any girl I want to go out with me because my name is Kennedy. I don't like it at all. But I guess I'd better get used to it, because once a Kennedy, always a Kennedy.

> —*Joseph P. Kennedy II. Remark to his grandfather's nurse, c. 1969.*

I can't do it the way they did. The conditions aren't the same. I've got to take shortcuts. . . . If you see your limits, you won't even reach them. To strive, to seek new worlds—that's what my father stressed.

> —*Robert F. Kennedy Jr. Remark to a friend on his decision to explore the Apurímac River in the Amazon.*

They have their own idea of reality, which isn't mine, but it has a hold on me.

> —*David Kennedy. Remark to interviewers after his family accused him of revealing the family's secrets in interviews.*

I had a confrontation with adolescence. And I had the same things poured into adolescence that a lot of other people do—I had parents who were separated and divorced, I had challenges. . . . I don't think I've got more added pressures than anyone else does. It's just more publicized. It doesn't matter whether it's because I'm a Kennedy or somebody who's like anybody else, facing feelings that are baffling to them.

The thing that I worry about being measured against most is my own family's internal measures. I'm not going to feel good or bad based on how I've been measured in a public medium.

> —*Patrick J. Kennedy. Remarks on his past during his campaign for U.S. representative from Rhode Island. Quoted in the* Washington Post, *June 7, 1994.*

When I say something, it's not simply Patrick speaking. I'm a Kennedy. It's a responsibility I have.

> —*Patrick J. Kennedy. Remark. Quoted in the* Boston Globe, *December 10, 1991.*

You feel it [public attention and expectation], and you're a little embarrassed by it, but there's not a lot you can do about it. A large part doesn't have anything to do with anything I've earned. It has to do with who I am. It's not like you're the quarterback of the team and threw the winning pass at the Super Bowl. So other congressmen feel that, and they are resentful.

> —*Joseph P. Kennedy II.*
> *Interview. Quoted in the*
> Boston Globe, *May 23, 1993.*

The Political Family

My babies were rocked to political lullabies.

> —*Rose Kennedy. Quoted in the*
> Washington Post Magazine,
> *April 29, 1990.*

I have no political ambitions for myself or my children.

> —*Joseph P. Kennedy.*
> *Introduction to* I'm for
> Roosevelt, *1936.*

I am going to feel that I'm out of politics—if this is politics—for the rest of my natural life. I'm all through with public life.

> —*Joseph P. Kennedy. Remarks*
> *to reporters after resigning his*
> *chairmanship of the SEC,*
> *September 21, 1935.*

If I had my eye on another job, it would be a complete breach of faith with President Roosevelt.

> —*Joseph P. Kennedy. Response*
> *to reporters who asked if he*
> *had presidential ambitions.*

I got Jack into politics. I was the one. I told him Joe [Jr.] was dead and that it was therefore his responsibility to run for Congress. He didn't want to. He felt he didn't have the ability and he still feels that way. But I told him he had to.

> —*Joseph P. Kennedy. Interview,*
> McCall's, *August 1957.*

It was like being drafted. My father wanted his eldest son in politics. "Wanted" isn't the right word. He demanded it. You know my father.

> —*John F. Kennedy. Remark,*
> *quoted in* New York Journal-
> American, *December 1, 1963.*

Jack doesn't belong anymore to a family. He belongs to the country. That's probably the saddest thing about all this. The family can be there, but there is not much they can do for the President of the United States.

> —*Joseph P. Kennedy. Interview,*
> New York Times, *January 8,*
> *1961.*

If Jack ever feels he has anything to ask me—I've had lots of different experiences in life—he knows where to find me, and I'll tell him what I think. But I feel very strongly about older children. I had a contract years ago with a couple of firms and all they paid me for was "for advice—when requested." That's the way it's going to be between my son and me.

> —*Joseph P. Kennedy. Remark*
> *after John F. Kennedy became*
> *president. Quoted in the* New
> York Journal-American,
> *January 8, 1961.*

No matter what the previous relationship had been, the moment a man sits behind the White House desk, from then on it is "Mr. President." I'm certainly not going to call my son "Mr. President" when we're alone together, but if there are people around we don't know very well I do, and it doesn't seem at all strange.

—*Joseph P. Kennedy. Interview,*
quoted in William Manchester,
Portrait of a President, *1962.*

Now, look here, Dad, you have your political views and I have mine. I'm going to vote exactly the way I feel I must on this!

—*John F. Kennedy. To his*
father, who insisted John cast
a particular vote on a bill in
the House, c. 1950.

I guess Dad has decided that he's going to be the ventriloquist, so I guess that makes me the dummy.

—*John F. Kennedy. Remark to*
friend Kirk Billings on his role
as a U.S. representative,
c. 1950.

Dad is a financial genius, all right, but in politics, he is something else.

—*John F. Kennedy. Quoted in*
Newsweek, *September 12,*
1960.

All this business about Jack and Bobby being blood brothers has been exaggerated. . . . They had different tastes in men, different tastes in women. They didn't really become close until 1952, and it was politics that brought them together.

—*Eunice Kennedy Shriver.*
Interview. Quoted in Margaret
Laing, The Next Kennedy, *1968.*

Goddamn it, Jack, I want to tell you once and for all . . . Bobby spilt his blood for you. He's worked for you. And goddamn it, he wants to be attorney general, and I want him to be attorney general, and that's it.

> —*Joseph P. Kennedy. Remark while John F. Kennedy was picking his appointments, December 1960.*

He [President Kennedy] asked me if I wanted to be attorney general. I said I didn't want to be attorney general. . . . In the first place, I thought nepotism was a problem. Secondly, I had been chasing bad men for three years and I didn't want to spend the rest of my life doing that.

> —*Robert F. Kennedy. Interview, February 1964.*

Nepotism, my foot! Why should anybody think that Bobby needs a job?

> —*Joseph P. Kennedy. Remark quoted in the* New York Journal-American, *January 8, 1961.*

If you announce me as attorney general, they'll kick your balls off.

> —*Robert F. Kennedy. Remark to John F. Kennedy on his planned appointment, December 1960.*

So that's it, gentlemen. Let's grab our balls and go.

> —*John F. Kennedy to his aides, two days later.*

When asked by a friendly journalist how he would announce Robert as attorney general, John Kennedy replied:

Well, I think I'll open the front door of the Georgetown house some morning about 2:00 A.M., look up and down the street, and, if there's no one there, I'll whisper, "It's Bobby."

> —*John F. Kennedy. December 1960.*

In this cabinet there really is no person with whom I have been intimately connected over the years. I need to know that when problems arise I'm going to have somebody who's going to tell me the unvarnished truth, no matter what . . . and Bobby will do that.

> —*John F. Kennedy. Remark to John Seigenthaler and Robert Kennedy, December 1960.*

I can't see that it's wrong to give him a little legal experience before he goes out to practice law.

> —*John F. Kennedy. Remark on appointing his brother U.S. attorney general, quoted in* Time, *February 3, 1961.*

Bobby we'll make attorney general so he can throw all the people Dad doesn't like into jail. They'll have to build more jails.

> —*Eunice Kennedy Shriver. Remark shortly after the presidential election, 1960.*

Robert Kennedy recorded the president's announcement of his attorney general pick:

He told me to go upstairs and comb my hair to which I said
it was the first time the President had ever told the Attorney
General to comb his hair before they made an announcement.
And then when we were outside he said, "Don't smile too
much or they'll think we're happy about the appointment."

> —Robert F. Kennedy.
> Memorandum, February 8,
> 1961.

I decided at quite a young age that I would . . . work for
the government.

> —Robert F. Kennedy. Remark
> during Judiciary Committee
> hearings on his appointment,
> January 13, 1961.

Years ago I was a hardworking lawyer making $4,200 a year.
I took my work home every night and was very diligent. Ten
years later I became the attorney general of the United States.
So you see, if you want to become successful, just get your
brother elected president.

> —Robert F. Kennedy. Speech to
> graduating class at Marquette
> University.

You boys have what you want now, and everybody else
helped you work to get it. Now it's Ted's turn. Whatever he
wants, I'm going to see he gets it.

> —Joseph P. Kennedy. Remarks
> to John and Robert. Quoted in
> Time, September 28, 1962.

In my family, we were interested not so much in the ideas of
politics as in the mechanics of the whole thing.

> —John F. Kennedy. Remark,
> quoted in Laurence Leamer,
> The Founding Father, 1964.

You know what this reminds me of? That scene in *Gone with the Wind* where Scarlett's colored servants move into Tara with her after the war. I feel like the old mammy who takes a look around and then says, "Man, we's rich now."

> —*Eunice Kennedy Shriver.*
> *Remark made on her first*
> *visit to the White House,*
> *January 20, 1961.*

If that girl had been born with balls, she would have been a hell of a politician.

> —*Joseph P. Kennedy on his*
> *daughter Eunice.*

I think every woman wants to be needed, and in politics, you are.

> —*Jacqueline Kennedy.*

I separate politics from my private life; maybe that's why I treasure my life at home so much.

> —*Jacqueline Kennedy. During*
> *the presidential campaign,*
> *1960.*

What I wanted to do more than anything [was to] keep my family together in the White House. I didn't want to go down into coal mines or be a symbol of elegance.

> —*Jacqueline Kennedy Onassis.*
> *Letter, June 1973.*

Journalist Laura Bergquist spent several days with the Kennedys during their activities outside and within the White House in 1961, taking pictures for Life. *Although Jackie at one point requested that she not take candid shots of Caroline playing, she was unable to resist. The photos were sent to Jack and Jackie for approval, and Jackie wrote back:*

You are right—they are such good pictures. . . . It is partly because they are so good I must sadly tell you I just can't give you permission to publish them. Caroline was being recognized wherever she went. That is a strange enough thing to get used to at any age—but pretty sad when one is only three. Every article just increases interest in her—her little friends and cousins see it and mention it to her and it is all bad for her.

> —*Jacqueline Kennedy. Letter to journalist Laura Bergquist, July 23, 1961.*

The one thing I do not want to be called is First Lady. It sounds like a saddle horse. Would you notify the telephone operators and everyone else that I'm to be known simply as Mrs. Kennedy and not as First Lady.

> —*Jacqueline Kennedy. Instructions to her secretary, 1961.*

Dad, I'm going to California for a few days and I'm going to fight hard. I'm going to win one for you.

> —*Robert F. Kennedy. To his sick father during the presidential primaries, 1968.*

My views on birth control are somewhat distorted by the fact that I was the seventh of nine children.

> —*Robert F. Kennedy. Remark.*

The thing about being a Kennedy is that you come to know there's a time for Kennedys. And it's hard to know when that time is, or if it will ever come again. . . . I mean, is the country going to be receptive? Will it be the time? And if it is, is it really the best thing for me to do? And how much of a contribution could I make, even if . . . ?

> —*Edward M. Kennedy. Quoted in* Time, *January 10, 1969.*

We have to measure what we are by what our parents were. Grandpa had things completely wired—Massachusetts, the whole of the East Coast. He had it under control. He was a political consultant, a political action committee, and a media consultant all rolled into one. His only client was his family. He was fanatically dedicated to making it happen. Nobody in this family is ever again going to decide that it's a life-or-death matter whether or not a Kennedy gets elected to something. Even if they did, they can't make it happen anymore. That's what's changed and we might as well accept it.

—Robert Sargent Shriver.
Remark to family members,
Thanksgiving 1982.

This is Joe Kennedy running for office . . . and no other member of my family.

—Joseph P. Kennedy II.
Announcing his bid for
congressman from
Massachusetts, December 4,
1985.

Has my family name helped me? Of course it's a big help to me. I'm the first to acknowledge it, and my colleagues who have supported me will readily acknowledge that, yes, I can certainly take advantage of the opportunity.

—Patrick J. Kennedy. Comment
on his family name during his
1994 campaign for U.S.
representative from Rhode
Island. Quoted in the
Christian Science Monitor,
August 29, 1994.

Husbands and Wives

At first I liked Mr. Kennedy, but I didn't love him. In time I came to love him very much. Very much.

> —*Rose Kennedy. Remark to her family, Thanksgiving 1982.*

I don't think he ever did ask me, not just straight out. It was less a matter of "Will you marry me?" than of "When we get married."

> —*Rose F. Kennedy. Writing on Joseph's proposal of marriage,* Times to Remember, *1974.*

The most thrilling, exciting, and interesting years of my life were the ones I spent in London when Joe was ambassador.

> —*Rose F. Kennedy. Personal papers.*

Its [sic] Hell to be here without all of you. . . . I get news that you are more beautiful than ever. Maybe you do better away from me. All my love.

> —*Joseph P. Kennedy. Letter to Rose Kennedy from London, April 26, 1940.*

I don't think I know anyone who has more courage than my wife. In all the years that we have been married, I have never heard her complain. Never. Not even once. . . . That is a quality that children are quick to see.

> —*Joseph P. Kennedy. Quoted in the* New York Herald Tribune, *December 12, 1960.*

Your father again has restricted my activities and thinks the little woman should confine herself to the home. Personally, I think it shows [an] antiquated system with emphasis made on the unessentials, and after all, there are times when a woman should show initiative. . . . (This is, of course, all in fun, and don't discuss it outside of the family circle.)

> —Rose Kennedy. Letter to her
> children, February 2, 1942.

Sometimes I feel that I am never going to take it [marriage] on. No one I have ever met ever made me completely forget myself and one cannot get married with that attitude.

> —Kathleen Kennedy. Letter to a
> friend, c. 1940.

How can I fight God?

> —Robert F. Kennedy. Remark
> when learning that his future
> wife was considering
> becoming a nun.

When she met John F. Kennedy, Jacqueline Bouvier was working as the "Inquiring Camera Girl" for the Washington Times-Herald, where it was her responsibility to ask light questions of figures around Washington, and take their picture. To John F. Kennedy, her questions were pointed:

Can you give any reason why a contented bachelor would want to get married?

> —Jacqueline Bouvier.

I'm the luckiest girl in the world. Mummy is terrified of Jack because she can't push him around.

> —Jacqueline Bouvier. Remark
> during her courtship with
> John F. Kennedy.

Since Jack is such a violently independent person, and I, too, am so independent, this relationship will take a lot of working out.

> —*Jacqueline Bouvier. Response to a reporter's question on what she and John F. Kennedy had in common, 1953.*

I don't think there are any men who are faithful to their wives. Men are such a combination of good and evil.

> —*Jacqueline Kennedy. Remark made early in her marriage to John F. Kennedy.*

We are like two icebergs—the public life above the water, the private life submerged. It is a bond between us.

> —*Jacqueline Kennedy. On her marriage with John F. Kennedy, undated letter to writer Fletcher Knebel.*

I wouldn't say that being married to a very busy politician is the easiest life to adjust to. But you think about it and figure out the best way to do things—to keep the house running smoothly, to spend as much time as you can with your husband and your children—and eventually you find yourself well adjusted. . . . The most important thing for a successful marriage is for a husband to do what he likes best and does well. The wife's satisfaction will follow.

> —*Jacqueline Kennedy. Interview, 1956.*

Since I'm completely committed [to the presidential campaign], and since she is committed to me, that commits her.

> —*John F. Kennedy. On Jackie's role in his presidential bid.*

Oh, bunny, you're president now!

> —*Jacqueline Kennedy. Remark*
> *to John F. Kennedy, 10:30*
> P.M., Election Day 1960.

I searched all my life for someone like my father, and Sarge came closest.

> —*Eunice Kennedy Shriver.*
> *Wedding toast to Sargent*
> *Shriver, 1953.*

The funny thing is that everyone thinks this is a marriage made in heaven. Both my mother- and father-in-law, and my parents and me, and all my girlfriends and Ted's friends. Everyone thinks this is a marriage that will be perfect.

> —*Joan Kennedy. Interview on*
> *her marriage to Edward*
> *Kennedy, quoted in Laurence*
> *Leamer,* The Kennedy
> Women, *1994. They were*
> *separated in 1980.*

For him, the world is divided into black and white hats. The white hats are for us and the black hats are against us. Bobby can only distinguish good men and bad, good things and bad. Good things, in his eyes, are virility, courage, movement, and anger. He has no patience with the weak and the hesitant.

> —*Ethel Kennedy on her*
> *husband, Robert F. Kennedy.*
> *Quoted in Harrison Rainie*
> *and John Quinn,* Growing up
> Kennedy.

How could I possibly do that? With Bobby looking down from heaven, that would be adultery.

> —*Ethel Kennedy. Remark to a*
> *friend on why she would not*
> *remarry, 1976.*

Parents on Children

After all, my wife and I have given nine hostages to fortune. Our children and your children are more important than anything else in the world. The kind of America that they and their children will inherit is of grave concern to us all.

> —*Joseph P. Kennedy. Radio address endorsing Roosevelt's third term, October 1940.*

I always felt that if the older children are brought up right, the younger ones will follow their lead.

> —*Rose Kennedy. Quoted by Joseph F. Dineen,* The Kennedy Family, *1959.*

I am much happier being the father of nine children and making a hole in one than I would be as the father of one making a hole in nine.

> —*Joseph P. Kennedy. Comment to the English press after making a hole in one at the Stokes Poges golf course in Buckinghamshire, 1938.*

I still insist that, whenever I leave England, whatever my record is, I shall still be known as the father of nine children.

> —*Joseph P. Kennedy. Remark to reporters. Quoted in the* Manchester Guardian, *May 18, 1939.*

I woke up one morning exhausted, and I realized that I hadn't been out of that hotel room in seven weeks. My baby, Pat, had been born and was almost a month old, and I hadn't even seen her.

> —*Joseph F. Kennedy. Remark on how his business had interfered with family life, 1924.*

I did not think it was vital for my husband to be on hand for the birth of the babies.

> —*Rose Kennedy.* Times to Remember, *1974.*

The measure of a man's success in life is not the money he's made. It's the kind of family he has raised.

> —*Joseph P. Kennedy. Frequent remark.*

My work is my boys.

> —*Joseph P. Kennedy. Answering a friend's question: "What are you doing these days?"*

The reason I am sometimes reluctant about extra goodies for the children is that I read once that youngsters should get used to a few disappointments or jolts when they are young. They thus build up an immunity against them, so that when they encounter life's vicissitudes when they are older, they are not too shocked and they can take them with a smile.

> —*Rose Kennedy. Letter to daughters-in-law, August 26, 1969.*

I think a lot depends on the oldest one, and how he turns out. The younger ones follow his example. If the oldest one is a playboy and spends all of his time at El Morocco, the other ones who come along are apt to follow his example and do the same thing. If the oldest one tries to set a good example, the other ones try to live up to it.

> —*Joseph P. Kennedy. Quoted in Ralph G. Martin and Ed Plaut,* Front Runner, Dark Horse, *1960.*

We don't want any losers around here. In this family we want winners. . . . Don't come in second or third—that doesn't count—but win.

> —*Joseph P. Kennedy. Quoted by Rose Kennedy,* Times to Remember, *1974.*

I strongly urge you to pay a little more attention to penmanship. Mine has always been pretty bad, so I am not a very good authority to speak about it, but yours is disgraceful and should get some attention.

> —*Joseph P. Kennedy. Letter to John F. Kennedy, October 10, 1934.*

Don't let me lose confidence in you again, because it will be pretty nearly an impossible task to restore it.

> —*Joseph P. Kennedy. Letter to John F. Kennedy, April 29, 1935.*

Now, Jack, I don't want to give the impression that I am a nagger, for goodness knows I think that is the worst thing any parent can be. After long experience in sizing up people I definitely know you have the goods and you can go a long way. Now aren't you foolish not to get all there is out of what God has given you. . . . After all, I would be lacking even as a friend if I did not urge you to take advantage of the qualities you have. It is very difficult to make up fundamentals that you have neglected when you were very young and that is why I am always urging you to do the best you can. I am not out to be a real genius, but I think you can be a really worthwhile citizen with good judgment and understanding.

> —*Joseph P. Kennedy. Letter to John F. Kennedy, 1934.*

I admit that with Teddy I did things a little differently than I did with the other children. He was my baby and—I think every mother will understand this—I tried to keep him my baby.

—*Rose Kennedy.*

I don't care what the boys think about my ideas. I can take care of myself; the important thing is that they fight together.

—*Joseph P. Kennedy. Reply to Rose's concern about Joe Jr. and Jack taking sides against him in lively political debates over dinner.*

The generation that follows me may have to stand for everything that I stood against—and I realize that includes even my own sons. I made my choice among philosophies offered when I was young. Each of them will have to make his or her choice.

—*Joseph P. Kennedy. Quoted in Joseph F. Dineen,* The Kennedy Family, *1959.*

Bobby is more direct than Jack. Jack has always been one to persuade people what to do . . . [Bobby] resembles me much more than any of the other children. . . . He's a great kid. He hates the same way I do.

—*Joseph P. Kennedy. Quoted in* Newsweek, *March 18, 1963.*

I've had a wonderful life. If I died tomorrow, I could leave each one of my children a million dollars. And you know, they'd never have as exciting a time as I've had.

—*Joseph P. Kennedy. Remark, 1939.*

I've got nine children, and the only thing I can leave them that will mean anything is my good name and reputation.

> —*Joseph P. Kennedy. Remark to a friend before he left to become ambassador to England, 1937.*

I don't know what is going to happen to this family when I die. There is no one in the entire family, except Joan and Teddy, who is living within his means. No one appears to have the slightest concern for how much they spend.

> —*Joseph P. Kennedy. Remark to his children, 1956.*

I have a strong idea that there is no other success for a father and mother except to feel that they have made some contributions to the development of their children.

> —*Joseph P. Kennedy. Letter following John F. Kennedy's election to president.*

Years ago we decided that our children were going to be our best friends and that we never could see too much of them. Since we couldn't do both, it was better to bring up our family than go out to dinners.

> —*Rose Kennedy. Interview, 1939.*

I saw [corporal punishment] as a duty, never to be done in anger or a fit of irritability. I'd just tell them not to do something and spank them with the ruler if they did it. If a child is walking with me on the sidewalk and runs in front of a passing car, I quickly paddle him then and there, and so he is not apt to run out again. If he goes near a stove which is hot, I hold his finger near the stove to show him he will be burned. Or if he takes my sharp scissors . . . I stick the point into his arm or finger to show the seriousness of such a point in the eye. If this reasoning does not avail, I used to have my ruler in my desk and would use it.

> —*Rose Kennedy. Oral History.*

He dances very well, has remarkable rhythm, and shakes his head like a veteran when he does the conga. He only fell down once last week, so he is improving.

> —Rose Kennedy. Comments on
> Edward Kennedy's progress in
> dance class at age nine. Letter
> to her children, February 16,
> 1942.

I do hope you are working harder, dearest Teddy. As I said before, the Kennedy boys worked hard and were usually at the top of their classes in Boston, and I am sure the first question most people ask about you is, "Are you smart like your father?"—not to mention that I graduated from good old Dorchester High School with honors myself—so please get on your horse.

> —Rose Kennedy. Letter to
> Edward Kennedy, April 18,
> 1945.

I hoped that Ted would grow up and become a priest or even a bishop. But he met a beautiful blonde one night, and that was the end of my hopes for Ted for clerical life.

> —Rose Kennedy. Campaigning
> for Edward Kennedy with his
> wife, Joan. Cardinal Cushing
> Central High School, Boston,
> 1960.

Well, I think their first duty is to their family, and I think it would be very difficult to do both.

> —Rose Kennedy. Reply when
> asked why she didn't urge her
> daughters to go into politics.
> Interview, The David Frost
> Show, July 5, 1971.

That's about the most beautiful baby boy I've ever seen. Maybe I'll name him Abraham Lincoln.

> —*John F. Kennedy. Remark on newborn John F. Kennedy Jr., November 25, 1960.*

During a meeting with Randolph Churchill over the future of the British Labour Party, John Jr. jumped out from a hiding place under his father's Oval Office desk and screamed: "I'm a big bear and I'm hungry." President Kennedy replied, "I'm a great big bear and I'm going to eat you up in one bite." He then turned to Churchill and responded to his puzzled expression:

You may think this is strange behavior in the office of the president of the United States, but in addition to being the President, I also happen to be a father.

> —*John F. Kennedy.*

A man without a child is incomplete.

> —*Jacqueline Kennedy. Remark on seeing the affection John F. Kennedy showed for his newborn daughter.*

People have too many theories about rearing children. I believe simply in love, security, and discipline.

> —*Jacqueline Kennedy, 1959.*

My major effort must be devoted to my children. If Caroline and John turn out badly, nothing I could do in the public eye would have any meaning.

> —*Jacqueline Kennedy. Remark shortly after moving into the White House, 1961.*

Children have imagination, a quality that seems to flicker out in so many adults. That is why it is such a joy to be with children.

> —*Jacqueline Kennedy. Remark, February 1961.*

If you bungle raising your children, I don't think whatever else you do well matters very much.

> —*Jacqueline Kennedy. Quoted in Theodore C. Sorenson, Kennedy, 1965.*

[Thomas Carlyle] said you should do the duty that lies nearest you. The thing that lies nearest me is the children.

> —*Jacqueline Kennedy. Remark after John F. Kennedy was killed.*

"Plane." "Good-bye." "New Hampshire." "Wisconsin." "West Virginia."

> —*Caroline Kennedy's first words, uttered while on the primary campaign trail with Jackie and her father, 1960.*

I am sorry so few states have primaries, or we would have a daughter with the greatest vocabulary of any two-year-old in the country."

> —*Jacqueline Kennedy. Remarking on Caroline saying her first words, May 1960.*

She [Caroline Kennedy] is at the age now where she misses him. I think he probably suffers as much as she does (though neither of them are probably as aware of it as I am) from his absence.

> —*Jacqueline Kennedy. Undated letter to writer Fletcher Knebel, c. 1960.*

I've seen the worst of everything, I've seen the best of everything. But I can't replace my family.

> —*Jacqueline Kennedy Onassis. Remark, 1981.*

President Kennedy and his family visited the Kennedy home in Hyannis Port, Cape Cod, before the president left for Europe to meet with Khrushchev for the first time. Arrangements were still being made by phone. The elder Kennedy, however, did not feel uncomfortable giving strong advice on parenting in the midst of history making:

Jack, I saw what happened outside. Caroline was in tears and came out. You had a call from the White House. I know there are a lot of things on your mind about your meeting with Khrushchev . . . but let me tell you something: Nothing that will happen during your presidency will be as important as how Caroline turns out. And don't forget it.

> —*Joseph P. Kennedy. Comment to John F. Kennedy, 1961.*

I get reacquainted with the youngsters every weekend.

> —*Robert F. Kennedy. Remark made during his investigation of labor practices, 1958.*

You are the oldest of all the male grandchildren. You have a special and particular responsibility now which I know you will fulfill. Remember all the things that Jack started—be kind to others that are less fortunate than we—and love our country.

> —*Robert F. Kennedy. Letter to his eldest son, Joseph P. Kennedy II, written the day of John F. Kennedy's funeral.*

While watching his children play, Robert Kennedy remarked to a friend:

It doesn't seem like much of a world they're going to inherit, does it? I can't help wondering if I'm doing all I should to keep it from going down the drain.

—*Robert F. Kennedy, 1967.*

I believe in discipline and when I say "don't do something," the kids know I mean it.

—*Ethel Kennedy. Interview, the New York Times, April 20, 1968.*

It really came down to a little conversation between me and my boys a year or so ago, where they pointed out that there was a Mother's Day and a Father's Day, but lo and behold, there was no Children's Day. And they thought this was an outrage.

—*Joseph P. Kennedy II. Statement to the House of Representatives proposing resolution to make October 8 National Children's Day.*

This has been a very painful day for me and my family. As a father, my principle obligation and deepest personal desire is to assist my children through the most difficult time in their lives.

—*Joseph P. Kennedy II. Speech announcing that he and his wife were separating, and that he would not run for governor of Massachusetts, 1990.*

Children on Parents

Upon repeatedly hearing his father, newly appointed ambassador to England, addressed as "Your Excellency," Edward Kennedy asked:

Is that your new name, Daddy?

> —Edward M. Kennedy. Quoted in the Daily Mail, London, March 17, 1938.

I don't know where I got my brains, but its [sic] quite evident that I received them neither from my father nor my mother.

> —Robert F. Kennedy. Letter to Rose Kennedy from Milton Academy on his own unremarkable grades, December 7, 1942.

She [Rose Kennedy] was great on self-improvement. She always saw to it that we read good books, had good conversation.

> —John F. Kennedy. Interview, Time, June 6, 1960.

We were to try harder than anyone else. We might not be the best, and none of us were, but we were to make the effort to be the best. "After you have done the best you can," he [Joseph] used to say, "the hell with it."

> —Robert F. Kennedy. Quoted in Edward Kennedy, The Fruitful Bough, 1965.

I think that if the Kennedy children amount to anything now or ever amount to anything, it will be due more to Joe's behavior and his constant example than to any other factor. He made the task of bringing up a large family immeasurably easier for my father and mother, for what they taught him, he passed on to us and their teachings were not diluted through him, but rather strengthened. . . .

> —*John F. Kennedy.* As We Remember Joe, *1945. A collection of writings to commemorate Joseph P. Kennedy Jr. after his death in World War II.*

I can feel Pappy's eyes on the back of my neck. When the war is over and you are out there in sunny California . . . I'll be back here with Dad trying to parlay a lost PT boat and a bad back into a political advantage. I'll tell you, Dad is ready right now and can't understand why Johnny boy isn't "all engines full ahead."

> —*John F. Kennedy. Remark to a friend, 1944.*

The great thing about Dad is his optimism and his enthusiasm and how he's always for you. He might not always agree with what I do, just as I don't always agree with him, but as soon as I do anything, there's Dad saying, "Smartest move you ever made. . . . We really got them on the run now."

> —*John F. Kennedy. Quoted in* Newsweek, *March 18, 1963.*

My father would be for me if I were running as head of the Communist party.

> —*John F. Kennedy. Remark to a reporter, 1960.*

Rose is the finest teacher we ever had. She made our home a university that surpassed any formal classroom in the exciting quest for knowledge. With her gentle games and questions, she could bring the farthest reaches of the university to our dinner table, or transform the daily headlines into new and exciting adventures in understanding.

> —*Edward M. Kennedy. Speech, Georgetown University, Washington, D.C., October 1, 1977.*

He [Joseph] always trusted experience as the greatest creator of character. My mother believed religion was.

> —*Eunice Kennedy Shriver.*
> *Comment on her father,* The
> Fruitful Bough, *1965.*

All the places and feelings and happiness that bind you to a family you love are something that you take with you no matter how far you go.

> —*Jacqueline Bouvier. Letter to*
> *her stepfather from her junior*
> *year abroad at the Sorbonne.*

I think I could entertain a king or queen with less apprehension than my mother, when there are other guests present.

> —*Jacqueline Kennedy. Remark*
> *shortly after marrying John F.*
> *Kennedy, 1954.*

What it really all adds up to is love. Not love as it is described with such facility in popular magazines, but the kind of love that is affection and respect, order and encouragement and support. Our awareness of this was an incalculable source of strength. And because real love is something unselfish and involves sacrifice and giving, we could not help but profit from it.

> —*Robert F. Kennedy on his*
> *father. Quoted in Edward M.*
> *Kennedy's eulogy to Robert,*
> *June 8, 1968.*

Daddy got in fights, but he would never hit anybody smaller. He was completely moral. He was never with another woman before he was married or afterward. He was completely moral.

> —*Robert F. Kennedy Jr.*
> *Interview at age thirty.*

When he came home from work, all of us would rush to the door and wrestle him down to the ground. We'd drag Mother over too, and we'd tickle-tumble him and each other, rolling on the floor, laughing and shouting, until he cried "enough."

Next morning, when he left, he never got away without another round of tickle-tumbling, which he endured happily. I guess that's why he always looked so rumpled when he got to the Department of Justice or his Senate office.

—*Kathleen Kennedy Townsend.*
Interview on her father,
Robert F. Kennedy, McCall's,
1988.

If you dropped one of his passes—he was always quarterback—you felt like keeping on running. He had this withering look. You'd get back in the middle and he'd say, "I'm going to throw to you again and you'd better catch it."

—*Bobby Shriver, Eunice*
Kennedy Shriver's son.
Remarks in an interview on
playing football with Robert
F. Kennedy.

To make sure we were in condition for athletics, Father had the Green Berets set up an obstacle course on the grounds. [Peals of laughter.] Can you believe it! Green Berets! We climbed ropes, jumped, ran, swung, and we toughened up all right.

—*Kathleen Kennedy Townsend.*
Interview on her father,
Robert F. Kennedy, McCall's,
1988.

I don't think of my parents as having spend "quality time" with us. I mean, I don't buy into that whole quality-time nonsense. . . . I don't have memories of like being left home alone without my parents. I have, in fact, an image of my parents having practically no social life at all other than us.

—*Maria Owings Shriver,*
daughter of Eunice and
Sargent Shriver. Interview.

I remember growing up when people would come up and say, "Oh, your daughter is so pretty." I can see my mother going, "Stop it, stop it," to them, and then turning to me and say: "Don't pay attention to that. It's your mind." And I always said to myself, "She's so weird."

> —*Maria Owings Shriver,*
> *daughter of Eunice and*
> *Sargent Shriver. Interview.*

Siblings

I love him not just because
I oughter
But also because blood runs
thicker than water

> —*Caroline Kennedy. From a*
> *poem on her brother written*
> *at age fourteen and sent to*
> *Rose Kennedy for Christmas*
> *1971.*

Boy, the only persons you can be sure of are your own flesh and blood and then we are not always sure of them.

> —*Kathleen Kennedy. Letter to*
> *John F. Kennedy, 1942.*

It was just a matter of fact that only the boys talked at the dinner table. But that has ceased. The girls talk now.

> —*John F. Kennedy. Interview,*
> *Time, June 6, 1960.*

It seems hard to believe that you've been married ten years. I think they must have been the very best decade of your lives. At the start, in 1942, we had other lives and we were seven people thrown together, so many little separate units that could have stayed that way. Now we are nine—and what you've given us and what we've shared has bound us all to each other for the rest of our lives.

> —*Jacqueline Bouvier. From the introduction to a book of poems written to commemorate the tenth wedding anniversary of her mother, Janet, who had given birth to two children, and her stepfather, Hugh Auchincloss, who had three children from a previous marriage.*

She changes her hair, but I don't think she does it to appeal to voters. She does it because she likes to.

> —*Eunice Kennedy Shriver. Response to reporter's question about Jackie's new hairstyle,* Newark News, *October 12, 1960.*

If a mosquito bit Jack Kennedy, the mosquito would die.

> —*Robert F. Kennedy. Comment on his brother's illnesses and sickly pallor.*

In a large, united family, the eldest brother is often looked upon with something closely akin to awe. Younger brothers and sisters regard him as the foundation stone of the family, and that is the way we all unconsciously regarded Joe. . . .

> —*Kathleen Kennedy.* As We Remember Joe, *1945.*

When you have older brothers and sisters, they're the ones who seem most important in the family and always get the best rooms and the first choice of boats, and all those things. . . .

> —*Rose Fitzgerald Kennedy. Remark to Edward M. Kennedy as a child.*

I was the seventh of nine children, and when you come from that far down you have to struggle to survive.

> —*Robert F. Kennedy. Quoted in William V. Shannon,* The Heir Apparent, *1967.*

I've got to take second spot to Bobby for now.

> —*Edward M. Kennedy. Remark to his Senate staff after Robert was elected to the Senate, 1964.*

Teddy is a better natural politician than any of us.

> —*Robert F. Kennedy. Remark, 1962.*

I guess there will always be a Rosemary.

> —*John F. Kennedy. A rare remark on his institutionalized sister, c. 1950.*

They're for *him.*

> —*Robert F. Kennedy. Remark made privately after a Senate campaign speech in which the crowd responded most to his references to, and quotes from, Jack.*

You know . . . finally I feel that I'm out from under the shadow of my brother. Now at least I feel that I've made it on my own. All these years I never really believed it was me that did it, but Jack.

> —*Robert F. Kennedy to a friend after he won the California primary. He was assassinated shortly afterward.*

Like my brothers before me, I pick up a fallen standard. Sustained by the memory of our priceless years together, I shall try to carry forward that special commitment to justice, to excellence, and to courage that distinguished their lives.

> —*Edward M. Kennedy. Speech*
> *shortly before the 1968*
> *Democratic Convention.*

Tragedy and Resiliency

There were no tears for Joe and me, not then. We sat awhile, holding each other close, and wept inwardly, silently.

> —*Rose Kennedy on the death of*
> *Joe Kennedy Jr. in World*
> *War II.*

The sudden death of young Joe and Kathleen, within a period of three years, has left a mark with me that I find very difficult to erase.

> —*Joseph P. Kennedy. Letter to*
> *Lord William Beaverbrook,*
> *July 27, 1948.*

It is the realization that the future held the promise of great accomplishments for Joe [Jr.] that has made his death so particularly hard for those who know him. His worldly success was so assured and inevitable that his death seems to have cut into the natural order of things.

> —*John F. Kennedy. As We*
> Remember Joe, *1945.*

JOY SHE GAVE JOY SHE HAS FOUND

> —*Kathleen Kennedy's*
> *headstone, Edensor, England.*

Oh, a gun. You never know what's hit you. A gunshot is the perfect way.

> —*John F. Kennedy. Answer to a friend's question of what he thought the best way would be to die, 1963.*

There have been so many crises in his life. He'll pull through.

> —*Eunice Kennedy Shriver. Remark to Sargent Shriver immediately after learning that John F. Kennedy had been shot.*

These things happen. It's not going to be anything serious. Don't worry. We'll be all right. You'll see.

> —*Rose Kennedy. Remark to her niece, Ann Gargan, after learning that John had been shot.*

An exchange between Jacqueline Kennedy and Caroline Kennedy after John Kennedy's funeral:

CAROLINE: Mommy, did they love Daddy?

JACKIE: Oh, yes, they loved Daddy.

CAROLINE: No, Mommy, they didn't love Daddy. If they loved Daddy, they'd never have done what they did to him. Do they love you?

JACKIE: Caroline, I didn't quite give you the right answer to your first question. They did love Daddy. Far more of them loved Daddy than love me, although many people love me too. But I know what you are thinking and I don't think we should be surprised that some people did not love Daddy. After all, not everybody loved Jesus, did they?

> —*From Reverend John Cavanaugh, CSC, Oral History.*

I will tell you one thing. They will never drag me out like a little old widow like they did Mrs. Wilson when President Wilson died. I will never be used that way.

> —*Jacqueline Kennedy. Remark to Charles Bartlett, November 1963.*

When this is over, I'm going to crawl into the deepest retirement there is.

> —*Jacqueline Kennedy. Interview with Theodore White, November 29, 1963.*

Did the CIA kill my brother?

> —*Robert F. Kennedy to CIA director John F. A. McCone.*

I thought they'd get one of us, but Jack, after all he'd been through, never worried about it. . . . I thought it would be me.

> —*Robert F. Kennedy, November 22, 1963.*

President Kennedy was more than just president of a country. He was the leader of young people everywhere. What he was trying to do was fight against hunger, disease, and poverty around the world. You and I as young people have a special responsibility to carry on the fight.

> —*Robert F. Kennedy. Speech to students at Wajeda University, Japan, December 1963.*

The Kennedys intend to stay in public life. Good luck is something you make, and bad luck is something you endure.

> —*Robert F. Kennedy. Response when asked by a reporter if the family, given their tragedies, would step out of the spotlight, June 1964.*

Somebody up there doesn't like us.

> —*Robert F. Kennedy. Remark to
> a friend after Edward
> Kennedy survived a plane
> crash, but punctured a lung
> and crushed several vertebrae.
> June 1964.*

If they want to get me, they'll get me. They got Jack.

> —*Robert F. Kennedy. Remark to
> the press, concerned about a
> possible attempt on his life
> during the presidential
> primaries, 1968.*

*According to witness testimony, Robert F. Kennedy's last words, as he
lay on the kitchen floor of the Ambassador Hotel, near aide Paul
Schrade, who had also been hit, were:*

Is Paul okay? Is everybody all right?

We shall honor him not with useless mourning and vain
regrets for the past but with firm and indomitable resolution
for the future: attempting to relieve the starvation of people
in this society, working to aid the disadvantaged and those
helpless inarticulate masses for whom he felt so deeply.

> —*Rose Kennedy. Speech
> thanking supporters for their
> sympathy after Bobby's
> death, 1968.*

I can't let go. If I let go, Ethel will let go, and my mother will
let go, and all my sisters will let go.

> —*Edward M. Kennedy. Remark
> on mourning Robert F.
> Kennedy, 1968.*

Daddy was very funny in church because he would embarrass all of us by singing very loud. Daddy did not have a very good voice. There will be no more football with Daddy, no more swimming with him, no more riding and no more camping with him. But he was the best father their [sic] ever was and I would rather have him for a father for the length of time I did than any other father for a million years.

—David A. Kennedy. Written in
a collection of letters about
Robert F. Kennedy that his
children wrote as a Christmas
present to Ethel Kennedy,
1968.

My brother need not be idealized, or enlarged in death beyond what he was in life, to be remembered simply as a good and decent man, who saw wrong and tried to right it, saw suffering and tried to heal it, saw war and tried to stop it.

—Edward M. Kennedy. Eulogy
to Robert F. Kennedy, June 8,
1968.

All I want if someone's going to blow my head off is just one swing at him first.

—Edward M. Kennedy. Remark
to friends after Robert's
death.

I'm not afraid to die. I'm too young to die.

—Edward M. Kennedy. To a
reporter asking him about
Bobby's death.

I hate this country. I despise America and I don't want my children to live here anymore. If they're killing Kennedys, my kids are number one targets. . . . I want to get out of this country.

—Jacqueline Kennedy. Remark
to a friend, 1968.

One must not be defeated, one must not be defeated.

> —*Rose Kennedy. To herself as she waited for word on Edward Kennedy Jr.'s bone cancer, 1973.*

Nobody's ever going to have to feel sorry for me.

> —*Rose Kennedy. Remark to Jacqueline Kennedy Onassis after Robert F. Kennedy's assassination and during her husband's illness.*

You see, we had a monopoly. We had money, talent, relationships with one another, we boasted of good looks. We had so much that these things just can't keep on.

> —*Rose Kennedy. Interview, 1990.*

Whatever is decided, whatever the future holds for me, I hope I shall be able to put this most recent tragedy behind me and make some future contribution to our state and mankind, whether it be in public or private life.

> —*Edward M. Kennedy. From his televised address in which he gave his version of the Chappaquiddick tragedy, and concluded by asking Massachusetts voters to decide if he should continue in the Senate, July 1969.*

This is what I say is life. Teddy has everything for him. He goes out one night in an accident and everything is smashed. It just seems—as I was reading last night from Shakespeare—just how much destiny decides.

> —*Rose Kennedy. Interview on Chappaquiddick.*

We're so goddamned good at taking care of everybody else's problems, but absolutely lousy at looking after our own.

> —*Eunice Kennedy Shriver.*
> *Remark to a friend with a*
> *drug problem whom she was*
> *helping, 1980.*

I have come to believe, more strongly than ever, that after people die they really do live on through those who love them.

> —*Caroline Kennedy Schlossberg.*

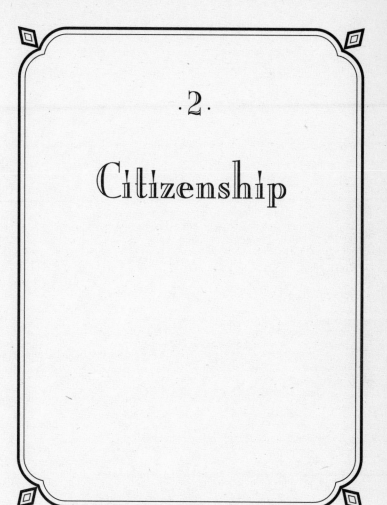

· 2 ·

Citizenship

Responsibilities and Sacrifices

Political action is the highest responsibility of a citizen.

> —*John F. Kennedy. Campaign speech, October 20, 1960.*

Are we up to the task? Are we equal to the challenge? Are we willing to match the Russian sacrifice of the present for the future? Or must we sacrifice our future in order to enjoy the present?

> —*John F. Kennedy. Acceptance speech, Democratic National Convention, Los Angeles, California, July 15, 1960.*

The real point about sacrifice, except in times of open warfare, is surely that it tends to be undramatic, prolonged, and irritating.

> —*Robert F. Kennedy. Speech, Joint Defense Appeal of the American Jewish Committee and the Anti-Defamation League of B'nai B'rith, Chicago, June 21, 1961.*

This country has really been built on the foundation that the government doesn't do everything; that neighbor helps his neighbor.

> —*Robert F. Kennedy. Speech, 1962.*

The Greek word *idiot* comes from that individual who didn't participate, who wasn't actively involved. President Kennedy's favorite quote was really from Dante: "The hottest places in hell are reserved for those who in time of moral crisis preserve their neutrality. . . ."

We have a special—not only responsibility—but a special opportunity to make a difference in the world, and make a difference for this country. . . . I think that we started three and a half years ago and I think that we can continue it. And I don't think it's just a question of political belief. I think that we can make a difference.

> —*Robert F. Kennedy. Question-and-answer session, Columbia/Barnard Democratic Club, New York City, October 5, 1964.*

Beneath it all he [Joseph P. Kennedy] has tried to engender a social conscience. There were wrongs which needed attention, there were people who were poor and needed help, and we have a responsibility to them and this country. Through no virtues and accomplishments of our own, we have been fortunate enough to be born in the United States under the most comfortable conditions. We therefore have a responsibility to others who are less well off.

> —*Robert F. Kennedy. Quoted in Edward M. Kennedy's eulogy to Robert, June 8, 1968.*

The idea of doing something for other people came from my parents. They both believed very strongly that those to whom much is given have responsibility. They both felt that we had a real responsibility for some kind of public service.

> —*Jean Kennedy. Interview.*

Let each of us, to the best of our ability, in our own day and generation, perform something worthy to be remembered. . . . Let us give something back to America, in return for all it has given us.

> —*Edward M. Kennedy. Speech, March 1, 1976.*

The American people care deeply about human rights around the world. But they also believe that human rights begin at home.

—Edward M. Kennedy. Speech,
June 9, 1977.

If I can leave a single message with the younger generation, it is to lash yourself to the mast, like Ulysses, if you want to escape the siren calls of complacency and indifference.

—Edward M. Kennedy. Speech,
June 4, 1978.

Community service is not a new idea in America. It is the essence of democracy. Throughout our history, we have dealt most effectively with the issues facing our country when we have come together to help one another.

—Edward M. Kennedy.
Statement, Judiciary
Committee hearing on the
Martin Luther King Holiday
and Service Act, April 13,
1994.

You can't sit back and enjoy the life that we in the United States, and my family in particular, have been born into, that is wealth, and any power that goes along with it. You have to go out and help others. You have to add something positive.

—Michael Lemoye Kennedy,
sixth child of Robert and
Ethel Kennedy and president
of the Citizens Energy
Corporation.

Rights, Freedoms, and Liberty

The rights of all men are diminished when the rights of any man are threatened.

> —*John F. Kennedy, 1961.*

Let us not be afraid of debate or discussion—let us encourage it. For if we should ever abandon these basic American traditions in the name of fighting communism, what would it profit us to win the whole world when we have lost our soul?

> —*John F. Kennedy. Address,*
> *National Civil Liberties*
> *Conference, Washington, D.C.,*
> *April 16, 1959.*

In times of clear and present danger, the courts have held that even the privileged rights of the First Amendment must yield to the public's need for national security.

> —*John F. Kennedy. Comment*
> *made ten days after the Bay*
> *of Pigs invasion, April 27,*
> *1961.*

The ideal of freedom has traveled a long and hard road through human history. Yet the record shows that the ideal persists and has an explosive power greater than that locked up within the atom.

> —*Robert F. Kennedy. Speech.*

In the election of 1860, Abraham Lincoln said the question was whether this nation could exist half-slave or half-free. In the election of 1960, and with the world around us, the question is whether the world will exist half-slave or half-free, whether it will move in the direction of freedom, in the direction of the road we are taking, or whether it will move in the direction of slavery. I think it will depend in great measure upon what we do here in the United States, on the kind of society that we build, on the kind of strength that we maintain.

—*John F. Kennedy. Opening statement, first Kennedy-Nixon debate, Chicago, September 26, 1960.*

It is one of the ironies of our time that the techniques of a harsh and repressive system should be able to instill discipline and ardor in its servants—while the blessings of liberty have too often stood for privilege, materialism, and a life of ease.

—*John F. Kennedy, comparing the societies of the United States and the Soviet Union. State of the Union Address, January 30, 1961.*

The free way of life proposes ends, but it does not prescribe means.

—*Robert F. Kennedy.* The Pursuit of Justice, *1964.*

If our constitution had followed the style of Saint Paul, the First Amendment might have concluded: "But the greatest of these is speech." In the darkness of tyranny, this is the key to the sunlight. If it is granted, all doors open. If it is withheld, none.

—*Robert F. Kennedy. Address, Tenth Anniversary Convocation, Center for Study of Democratic Institutions of the Fund for the Republic, New York City, January 22, 1963.*

Freedom by itself is not enough. "Freedom is a good horse," said Matthew Arnold, "but a horse to ride somewhere." What counts is how the use of liberty becomes the means of opportunity and growth and justice.

—*Robert F. Kennedy. Speech,
1964.*

As long as men are not free—in their lives and their opinions, their speech and their knowledge—that long will the American Revolution not be finished.

—*Robert F. Kennedy.
Commencement Address,
Queens College, New York
City, June 15, 1965.*

We are not against any man—or any nation—or any system—except as it is hostile to freedom.

—*John F. Kennedy. Address to
Congress, May 25, 1961.*

Although the Fifth Amendment is for the innocent as well as the guilty, I can think of very few witnesses who availed themselves of it who in my estimation were free of wrongdoing.

—*Robert F. Kennedy. The
Enemy Within, 1960.*

VOTING

If we can lower the voting age to nine, we are going to sweep the state.

—*John F. Kennedy. Campaign
speech, Girard, Ohio,
October 9, 1960.*

The most precious and powerful right in the world, the right to vote in a free American election, must not be denied to any citizen on grounds of his race or color. I wish that all qualified Americans permitted to vote were willing to vote, but surely in this centennial year of emancipation, all those who are willing to vote should always be permitted.

> —John F. Kennedy. State of the
> Union Address, Washington,
> D.C., January 14, 1963.

The ignorance of one voter in a democracy impairs the security of all.

> —John F. Kennedy. Speech,
> Vanderbilt University,
> Nashville, Tennessee, May 18,
> 1963.

From the vote, from participation in the elections, flow all other rights far, far more easily.

> —Robert F. Kennedy. Interview,
> December 1964.

The time has come to lower the voting age to eighteen in the United States, and thereby bring our youth into the mainstream of the political process. I believe this is the most important single principle we can pursue if we are to succeed in bringing our youth into full and lasting participation in our institutions of democratic government.

> —Edward M. Kennedy,
> February 23, 1970.

PRIVACY

My feeling is that the use of legal wiretaps should be limited to major crimes such as treason, kidnapping, and murder. . . . Legalized wiretapping is a two-edged sword that requires the most scrupulous use. For that reason, I would not be in favor of its use under any circumstances—even with the court's permission—except in certain capital cases.

—*Robert F. Kennedy. Interview,* Look, *March 22, 1961.*

Wiretapping is a subject of deepest concern to me. I do not believe in it. But I also believe we must recognize that there are two sides to the argument. In this regard it is interesting to note that when we introduced proposals revising the law on wiretapping, I found that many critics had not even bothered to read the bill. I was further interested by the fact that the American Civil Liberties Union strenuously opposed the bill, while the ACLU's own president, former Attorney General Biddle, testified in favor of it.

—*Robert F. Kennedy. Speech, 1964.*

We need more effective safeguards to ensure that every American can fully exercise his constitutional right to privacy. We must protect American citizens against the compiling of inaccurate or unverified data and the unrestricted use and dissemination of such data. . . . Experience has shown that as the capacity to store and disseminate personal information has increased through the use of computers and other devices, information has been collected to fill this capacity, to the detriment of the right to privacy.

—*Edward M. Kennedy. Speech, June 12, 1974.*

Human Nature

Men and women with freed minds may often be mistaken, but they are seldom fooled. They can be influenced, but they can't be intimidated. They may be perplexed, but they will never be lost.

—*Robert F. Kennedy. Speech, commencement exercises, Trinity College, Washington, D.C., June 2, 1963.*

When things are done on too vast a scale, the human imagination bogs down. It can no longer visualize such fantastic things and thus loses its grip on their essential reality. Killing one man is murder; killing millions is a statistic. . . . Our problems, having grown to the size of the world, if not of the solar system, no longer seem our own. Each day we are required to respond to new crises created by people whose names we cannot pronounce in lands of which we have never heard. After a time, the capacity to respond begins to flag; and we turn, not cheerfully, but almost in despair, to the sports pages and the comics.

—Robert F. Kennedy. Speech,
Joint Defense Appeal of the
American Jewish Committee
and the Anti-Defamation
League of B'nai B'rith,
Chicago, June 21, 1961.

A man does what he must—in spite of personal consequences, in spite of obstacles and dangers and pressures—and that is the basis of all human morality.

—John F. Kennedy. Profiles in
Courage, *1956.*

What is objectionable, what is dangerous about extremists is not that they are extreme, but that they are intolerant. The evil is not what they say about their cause, but what they say about their opponents.

—Robert F. Kennedy. The
Pursuit of Justice, *1964.*

What is it that men want? Isn't it freedom of conscience and action conditioned only by the legitimate needs of private and public security?

—Robert F. Kennedy. Speech,
Tenth Anniversary
Convocation, Center for Study
of Democratic Institutions of
the Fund for the Republic, New
York City, January 22, 1963.

The individual man, in whose hands democracy must put its faith and its fate, is capable of great heights of achievement. He is also capable of infinite degradation. Fortunately, most of our institutions have safeguards which ultimately unseat a man when power results in arrogance and corruption. But often before justice is done, the very institutions and values by which we attempt to order our lives can be undermined.

—*Robert F. Kennedy. Speech, 1964.*

I believe in human dignity as the source of national purpose, in human liberty as the source of national action, in the human heart as the source of national compassion, and in the human mind as the source of our invention and our ideas.

—*John F. Kennedy. Acceptance Speech for New York Liberal party nomination, September 14, 1960.*

Few men are willing to brave the disapproval of their fellows, the censure of their colleagues, the wrath of their society. Moral courage is a rarer commodity than bravery in battle or great intelligence. Yet it is the one essential, vital quality for those who seek to change a world which yields most painfully to change.

—*Robert F. Kennedy. Speech, Day of Affirmation, University of Capetown, June 6, 1966.*

Every society is a mixture of stability and change, an irrevocable history and an uncertain future. We are both what we have been and what we desire to be. We are creatures of memory and hope, struggling with uncertainty as we try to fulfill the promises that we know we must keep.

Thus our society is constantly in flux—different today from what it was yesterday—a continuation of the past, part of an organic process with roots deep in the history of our nations and of our common ancestors. Societies are like rivers, flowing from fixed and ancient sources through channels cut over the centuries—yet no man can ever step in the same water in which he stood only a moment ago.

> —*Edward M. Kennedy. Speech, Trinity College Historical Society Bicentennial, Dublin, Ireland, March 3, 1970.*

Leadership

Leaders are responsible for their failures only in the governing sector and cannot be held responsible for the failure of a nation as a whole.

> —*John F. Kennedy.* Why England Slept, *1940.*

He [a political leader] is also supposed to look after the national welfare, and to attempt to educate the people.

> —*Joseph P. Kennedy. Letter to John F. Kennedy on his manuscript of* Why England Slept, *1939.*

I am telling you what you are entitled to know: that my decisions on every public policy will be my own—as an American, a Democrat, and a free man.

After Buchanan this nation needed a Lincoln—after Taft, we needed a Wilson—after Hoover we needed Franklin Roosevelt—and after eight years of drugged and fitful sleep, this nation needs strong, creative Democratic leadership in the White House.

> —*John F. Kennedy. Acceptance speech, Democratic National Convention, Los Angeles, California, July 15, 1960.*

It is time for a new generation of leadership to cope with new problems and new opportunities. For there is a world to be won.

—*John F. Kennedy. Quoted in* Time, *November 6, 1989.*

In a world of complex and continuing problems, in a world full of frustrations and irritations, America's leadership must be guided by the lights of learning and reason—or else those who confuse rhetoric with reality and the plausible with the possible will gain the popular ascendancy with their seemingly swift and simple solutions to every world problem.

—*John F. Kennedy. Undelivered speech, Dallas, Texas, November 22, 1963.*

We do not need more study. We do not need more analysis. We do not need more rhetoric. What we need is more leadership and more commitment.

—*Edward M. Kennedy. Speech, July 27, 1972.*

Patriotism

I wonder what satisfaction any living person can be getting out of believing that this war will accomplish any of the things they thought it would accomplish. The so-called fight for Democracy and for Liberty will enslave every nation in the world, and leave them nothing of either Democracy or Liberty. . . . I get sick to my stomach when I listen to all the drivel that is being poured out to the American public.

—*Joseph P. Kennedy. Letter to Rose Kennedy, September 10, 1940.*

For Christ's sake, stop trying to make this a holy war, because no one will believe you. You're fighting for your life as an empire, and that's good enough.

> —*Joseph P. Kennedy, reacting to English arguments about protecting democracy from Hitler.*

No greater love has a man than he who gives his life for his brother.

> —*John F. Kennedy. Armistice Day speech to the Veterans of Foreign Wars, 1946.*

It [becoming a hero] was involuntary. They sank my boat.

> —*John F. Kennedy. Remark on his experience on PT 109.*

Let our patriotism be reflected in the creation of confidence rather than crusades of suspicion. Let us prove we think our country great by striving to make it greater. And, above all, let us remember that, however serious the outlook, the one great irreversible trend in world history is on the side of liberty—and so, for all time to come, are we.

> —*John F. Kennedy. Speech, Los Angeles, November 18, 1961.*

Came to the conclusion today that if I were an Englishman I would be very proud of so being.

> —*Robert F. Kennedy. Letter to his parents from Europe, June 30, 1948.*

Ever since the onset of the Cold War, we have been urged to "develop" a concise, exciting American manifesto—a platform which would compete with the simple, rousing calls of the communists. Such an effort, I think pointless—for what matters about this country cannot be put into simple slogans; it is a process, a way of doing things and dealing with people, a way of life. There are two major ways to communicate what this country is really about: to bring people here, or to send Americans abroad.

> —*Robert F. Kennedy. Speech, Sixth Annual West Side Community Conference, Columbia University, New York City, March 12, 1966.*

Perhaps never before in the history of the world has there been an emblem so full of the great aspirations of all men everywhere as the flag of the United States. . . . The flag our forebears received at their citizenship ceremony initiated them into the life of love and freedom, and they went forth to build a new nation. Our common aspirations today are as boundless as the mind of man. . . . They exceed even the deepest divisions of our time, because they reflect the timeless quest of men to be free, to live in a society that is open, where the principles of freedom and justice and equality prevail.

It is for this reason that patriotism and the flag can never be the special preserve of any particular party or any particular political philosophy. I love the flag no less because I believe that America has lost its way in Vietnam. I love the flag no less because I want America to move ahead to right the wrongs we see in our society at home. Those of us who push America on do so out of love and hope for the America that can be.

> —*Edward M. Kennedy. Fourth of July address, Wakefield, Massachusetts, July 4, 1970.*

As a nation, we have no hereditary institutions, and a minimum of ceremonial schools. The Constitution itself is our national symbol—the symbol of our identity, our continuity, and also our diversity.

It requires a mature people, mature in intelligence and political understanding, to respect that kind of abstract symbol, rather than the more tangible or human symbols of other nations.

—Edward M. Kennedy. Speech,
September 22, 1978.

·3·

American Society

The American Character

The American is by nature optimistic.

> —*John F. Kennedy. Quoted on NBC, Real Life, April 13, 1991.*

The United States has to move very fast to even stand still.

> —*John F. Kennedy. Quoted in the Observer, July 21, 1963.*

I go as the leader of the most revolutionary country on earth.

> —*John F. Kennedy. Speech to Massachusetts state Democrats on the eve of his first presidential trip to Europe, May 29, 1961.*

Let the word go forth from this time and place, to friend and foe alike, that the torch has been passed to a new generation of Americans—born in this century, tempered by war, disciplined by a hard and bitter peace, proud of our ancient heritage—and unwilling to witness or permit the slow undoing of those human rights to which this nation has always been committed, and to which we are committed today at home and around the world.

> —*John F. Kennedy. Inaugural address, January 20, 1961.*

When we got into office, the thing that surprised me most was to find that things were just as bad as we'd been saying they were.

> —John F. Kennedy. Speech at a
> dinner honoring his forty-
> fourth birthday, May 27,
> 1961.

If I were to send you a short summary of the whole situation in the country, I would just say "confusion."

> —Joseph P. Kennedy. Letter,
> December 1933.

On the bright side of an otherwise completely black time was the way that everyone stood up to it. Previous to that I had become somewhat cynical about the American as a fighting man. I had seen too much bellyaching and laying off. But with the chips down—that all faded away. I can now believe—which I never would have done before—the stories of Bataan and Wake. For an American it's got to be awfully easy or awfully tough. When it's in the middle, then there's trouble.

> —John F. Kennedy. Letter from
> PT 109 on his crew's bravery
> while stranded on a Japanese-
> held island, September 12,
> 1943.

Most of the courage shown in the war came from men's understanding of their interdependence on each other.

> —John F. Kennedy. Remark on
> his experiences in World War
> II.

The great events of which we are proud were forged by men who put their country above self-interest—their ideals above self-profit.

> —Robert F. Kennedy. Speech,
> University of Notre Dame,
> 1958.

As Edward Kennedy was campaigning for the Senate, the Boston Globe *broke the story of his expulsion from Harvard for cheating. John F. Kennedy, who was not in favor of the campaign to begin with, commented on the damage:*

It won't go over well with the WASPs. They take a dim view of looking over your shoulder at someone else's exam paper. They go in more for stealing from stockbrokers and banks.

— *John F. Kennedy.*

It seems to me imperative that we reinstall in ourselves the toughness and idealism that guided the nation in the past.

— *Robert F. Kennedy.* The
Enemy Within, *1960.*

The responsibility of our time is nothing less than to lead a revolution—a revolution which will be peaceful if we are wise enough; human if we care enough; successful if we are fortunate enough—but a revolution which will come whether we will it or not. We can affect its character: we cannot alter its inevitability. . . . America is, after all, the land of becoming— a continent which will be in ferment as long as it is America, a land which will never cease to change and grow. We are as we act. We are the children and the heirs of revolutions and we fulfill our destiny only as we advance the struggle which began in Santa Fe in 1580, which continued in Philadelphia in 1776 and Caracas in 1811—and which continues today.

— *Robert F. Kennedy. Speech
before Peruvian students,
1965.*

All of us, from the wealthiest to the young children that I have seen in this country . . . bloated by starvation—we all share one precious possession, that is the name *American.*
It is not easy to know what that means.

— *Robert F. Kennedy. Speech,
Citizens Union, New York
City, December 14, 1967.*

It is the young who have often been the first to speak and act against injustice or corruption or tyranny, wherever it is found. More than any other group in the population, it is the young who refuse to allow a difficulty or a challenge to become an excuse to fail to meet it. We need their ideas and ideals, the spirit and dedication of young Americans who are willing to hold a mirror to society and probe the sores that others would ignore.

—Edward M. Kennedy. Speech,
February 9, 1976.

I for one would not be happy to see this nation bland and homogeneous, its speech and literature reduced to the common denominator of mass-circulation magazines, its life settled down into a uniform suburb stretching from coast to coat. What would *Abie's Irish Rose* have been if Abie was Jewish and Rose Irish in *name* only?

—Robert F. Kennedy. Irish
Institute, April 1, 1967.

Not since the founding of the Republic—when Thomas Jefferson wrote the Declaration of Independence at thirty-two, Henry Knox built an artillery corps at twenty-six, Alexander Hamilton joined the independence fight at nineteen . . . has there been a younger generation of Americans brighter, better educated, more highly motivated than this one.

—Robert F. Kennedy. To Seek a
Newer World, *1967.*

Our future may lie beyond our vision, but it is not completely beyond our control. It is the shaping impulse of America that neither fate nor nature nor the irresistible tides of history, but the work of our own hands, matched to reason and principle, that will determine destiny. There is pride in that, even arrogance, but there is also experience and truth. In any event, it is the only way we can live.

—Robert F. Kennedy. To Seek a
Newer World, *1967.*

There is something basically wrong with America right now. We are not ourselves. Unhappiness, negativism, "againstness," seems to be the predominant current. Everybody is against something—against the war, against the students, against the president, against the press. We spend most of our time and energy and reaction being against. We do not chart courses, we plan battles. We do not have goals, we have targets. We do not work together, we choose up sides. We do not act, we react.

> —*Edward M. Kennedy.*
> *Commencement address,*
> *Manhattanville College, May*
> *30, 1970.*

What I think is quite clear is that we can work together in the last analysis, and that what has been going on within the United States over a period of the last three years—the division, the violence, whether it's between blacks and whites, between the poor and the more affluent, or between age groups or on the war in Vietnam—is that we can start to work together. We are a great country, an unselfish country, and a compassionate country.

> —*Robert F. Kennedy. Speech at*
> *the Ambassador Hotel after*
> *winning the California*
> *primary, and immediately*
> *before he was murdered, June*
> *4, 1968.*

The United States didn't grow for two hundred years to arrive in an atmosphere of turmoil and self-doubt. Somewhere, somehow, we have lost our way. Somewhere, somehow, in the past decade we lost sight of our own greatness and the promises that the American Revolution made to the world.

> —*Edward M. Kennedy. Speech,*
> *Boston Taxi Industry*
> *Scholarship Fund Dinner,*
> *Boston, June 17, 1970.*

Traveling across the length and breadth of America, taking the measure of our people, you cannot help but come away with a sense that we can do the job—that our problems are only human, and the solutions will be human, too; that America is a land whose people have the capacity to solve its problems many times over, if only we let them try.

> —*Edward M. Kennedy. Speech,*
> *National Jaycees Convention,*
> *Portland, Oregon, June 15,*
> *1971.*

It is not by accident that America over the years has been able to combine the wisdom of Athens and the might of Sparta. We have been a nation thrice blessed—blessed once with abundant natural resources; blessed a second time with a resourceful and stubborn citizenry . . . blessed a third time with a system of self-government that has reconciled, perhaps more perfectly than any other nation in history, the aspirations of individual freedom with the requirements of social order.

> —*Edward M. Kennedy. Speech,*
> *April 30, 1979.*

Eunice Kennedy Shriver described herself as a social liberal and a moral conservative. For example, she vehemently opposed abortion, but was committed to structuring society in such a way that women could more easily choose to have children. She saw those who stuck to only one side of the equation as contributing to the "hard society."

I would define the Hard Society as one without love—where everyone takes care of himself, where people use one another to satisfy their desires, but do not get involved with one another, because they do not want the responsibilities that go with permanent or deep relationships. . . . It is a society characterized by separateness between rich and poor, between whites and blacks, between an intellectual elite and the unlearned masses, where both individuals and blocs are concerned solely with maximizing their own comforts and enforcing their own prejudices.

> —*Eunice Kennedy Shriver.*
> *Article written for* Vogue, *May*
> *1969.*

Liberals and Conservatives

[The world "liberal"] has become entirely suspect because of the grossest sins committed in its name. Today many so-called leaders are professional liberals. They would rather be known as liberals than to be right. They have tortured a great word to cover a false philosophy, to wit, that the end justifies the means. Liberalism . . . has never meant a slavish devotion to a program, but rather did liberalism connote a state of the spirit, a tolerance for the views of others, an attitude of respect for others.

> —*Joseph P. Kennedy. Speech,*
> *Oglethorpe University,*
> *Atlanta, May 1941.*

There has been scarcely a liberal piece of legislation during the last sixty years that has not been opposed as communistic.

> —*Joseph P. Kennedy. Address,*
> *Democratic Businessmen's*
> *League of Massachusetts,*
> *October 24, 1936.*

Harry, how the hell could any son of mine be a goddamned liberal? Don't worry about Jack being a weak sister, he'll be tough.

> —*Joseph P. Kennedy. Response*
> *to concerns of Henry R. Luce,*
> *editor in chief of Time, Inc.,*
> *over how his conservative*
> *organization would report on*
> *Jack's liberal bent.*

Asked how he would answer those who said he was not a "true" liberal, John F. Kennedy replied:

I'd be happy to tell them that I'm not a liberal at all. I'm a realist.

—*John F. Kennedy. Quoted in the* Saturday Evening Post, *June 13, 1953.*

What do our opponents mean when they apply to us the label "liberal"? If by "liberal" they mean, as they want people to believe, someone who is soft in his policies abroad, who is against local government, and who is unconcerned with the taxpayer's dollar, then the record of this party and its members demonstrates that we are not that kind of "liberal." But if by a "liberal" they mean someone who looks ahead and not behind, someone who welcomes new ideas without rigid reactions, someone who cares about the welfare of the people . . . someone who believes we can break through the stalemate and suspicions that grip us in our policies abroad, if that is what they mean by a "liberal," then I'm proud to stay I'm a "liberal."

. . . For liberalism is not so much a party creed or set of fixed platform promises as it is an attitude of mind and heart, a faith in man's ability through the experiences of his reason and judgment to increase for himself and his fellow men the amount of justice and freedom and brotherhood which all human life deserves.

—*John F. Kennedy. Acceptance speech for New York Liberal party nomination, September 14, 1960.*

Some people have their liberalism "made" by the time they reach their late twenties. I didn't. I was caught in crosscurrents and eddies. It was only later that I got into the stream of things.

—*John F. Kennedy. Quoted in James MacGregor Burns,* John Kennedy: A Politician Profile, *1961.*

Most of us are conditioned for many years to have a political viewpoint—Republican or Democratic, liberal, conservative, or moderate. The fact of the matter is that most of the problems . . . that we now face are technical problems, are administrative problems. They are very sophisticated judgments, which do not lend themselves to the great sort of passionate movements which have stirred this country so often in the past. [They] deal with questions which are now beyond the comprehension of most men.

—John F. Kennedy. Press
conference, May 1962.

There is nothing "liberal" about a constant expansion of the federal government, stripping citizens of their public power—the right to share in the government of affairs—that was the founding purpose of this nation. There is nothing "conservative" about standing idle while millions of fellow citizens lose their lives and their hopes, while their frustration turns to fury that tears the fabric of society and freedom.

—Robert F. Kennedy. Address,
press luncheon, San
Francisco, May 21, 1968.

People are making too much of my so-called conversion to liberalism. I was liberal when I pardoned Junius Scales in 1962. But liberals had an emotional thing about me, maybe because of McCarthy, maybe because of my Roman Catholicism, maybe because of my fights with Humphrey and Stevenson. I'm not that different now. I know more now and I stay up late at night more often thinking about these problems. But I was never all that ruthless, as the liberals said.

—Robert F. Kennedy, May
1966.

To say that the future will be different from the present and past may be hopelessly self-evident. I must observe regretfully, however, that in politics it can be heresy. It can be denounced as radicalism or branded as stubborn. There are people in every time and every land who want to stop history in its tracks. They fear the future, mistrust the present, and invoke the security of a comfortable past which, in fact, never existed. It hardly seems necessary to point out that in the United States, of all places, that change, although it involves risk, is the law of life.

—Robert F. Kennedy. Speech, 1964.

I would say that a genuine conservative or a genuine liberal sees that there may be more than one way to resolve a particular issue. And he is willing to engage in discussion and listen to the views of others about what should be done.

—Robert F. Kennedy. Television interview, May 15, 1966.

I believe that extremists of both the right and the left share certain characteristics. They are totally intolerant of the views of others and totally unwilling to engage in discussion. They don't have to because they have a simple answer for every problem.

—Robert F. Kennedy. Television interview, May 15, 1966.

The challenges we face will require important changes in the structure of our institutions. It will not be easy to fit these changes into old categories—liberal or conservative, radical or reactionary. Instead they will bring to our public life new meanings for old words in our political dialogue—words such as "power," "community," and "purpose."

—Edward M. Kennedy. Speech, May 14, 1978.

Equality, Minorities, and Women

When the history of these times has been written, I hope and pray it will show that the American lads of 1941 did not pave the way for a radical change by fostering class antagonisms . . . and that they realized and took vigorous steps to spread the gospel of equality.

> —*Joseph P. Kennedy. Speech,*
> *Oglethorpe University,*
> *Atlanta, May 1941.*

It is my position that all students should be given the opportunity to attend public schools regardless of their race, and that is in accordance with the Constitution. It is in accordance, in my opinion, with the judgment of the people of the United States.

> —*John F. Kennedy. Press*
> *conference, February 8, 1961.*

There is always inequality in life. Some men are killed in war and some men are wounded and some men never leave the country. Life is unfair.

> —*John F. Kennedy. Speech,*
> *March 21, 1962.*

The poor man—the Negro, the Puerto Rican, the Spanish-American, the poor white—serves in Vietnam out of all proportion to his place in the population figures. And the casualty lists reflect disproportionate numbers of the poor as well. The Negroes and the poor in general bear the brunt of the fighting. We must intensify our efforts [toward equal rights] at home, for we must keep faith with the sacrifice they are making.

> —*Robert F. Kennedy. Speech,*
> *Third Annual WGHQ Human*
> *Relations Award Dinner,*
> *Ellenville, New York, April 19,*
> *1966.*

The time has long since arrived when loyal Americans must measure the impact of their actions beyond the limits of their own towns or states. For instance, we must be quite aware of the fact that 50 percent of the countries in the United Nations are not white; that around the world, in Africa, South America, and Asia, people whose skins are a different color than ours are on the move to gain their measure of freedom and liberty . . . and those people will decide not only their future but how the cause of freedom fares in the world. . . . In [the United Nations] and elsewhere around the world, our deeds will speak for us.

> —*Robert F. Kennedy. Law Day exercises, University of Georgia Law School, May 6, 1961.*

It is important to remember that in many areas of the United States there is no prejudice.

> —*Robert F. Kennedy. Voice of America broadcast, May 26, 1961.*

The greatest truth must be recognition that in every man, in every child, is the potential for greatness—that all are the creatures of God and equal in his sight.

> —*Robert F. Kennedy. Statement to Peruvian students, November 1965.*

Civil Rights remains the unfinished business of America.

> —*Edward M. Kennedy. Policy statement on civil rights legislation.*

The bitter fights of the Reagan-Bush years [over civil rights] left their mark on the social fabric of our country. Diversity— *E pluribus unum*—"Out of many, one"—is not just a slogan on our coins, but the founding political principle of our nation.

Too often in those years, it was replaced by the politics of division, and progress was far more difficult than it should have been.

> —*Edward M. Kennedy. Remarks on civil rights, October 22, 1993.*

NATIVE AMERICANS

Indians have heard fine words and promises long enough. They are right in asking for deeds.

> —*John F. Kennedy. Letter to Oliver La Farge of the Association on American Indian Affairs, 1960.*

From time to time in this nation's history attention is focused on the American Indian as though he had just arrived on our shores with new problems never before contemplated by government. There is a public cry for action. The wheels of government begin to churn. Congress and the executive branch deliberate, and then issue nice phrases. Finally, the difficulty of the task overwhelms us, our sense of immediacy fades, our indignation wanes, and the Indian "problem" is shelved for another generation.

> —*Edward M. Kennedy. Speech, July 12, 1978.*

I wish I'd been born an Indian.

> —*Robert F. Kennedy. Remark to Senator Fred Harris, whose wife is Comanche. Fred Harris Oral History, JFK Library.*

AFRICAN-AMERICANS AND THE CIVIL RIGHTS MOVEMENT

I won't say I stayed awake nights worrying about civil rights before I became attorney general.

> —*Robert F. Kennedy. Interview, Look, March 22, 1961.*

*After the summit with Khrushchev, President Kennedy was still some-
what wary about the repercussions of the freedom rides. When asked
for his view on the "freedom riders movement" in a press conference,
he avoided the issue of desegregation:*

. . .We believe that everyone who travels, for whatever
reason they travel, should enjoy the full constitutional protection given to them by the law and by the Constitution. They
should be able to move freely in interstate commerce. . . .
So the basic question is not the freedom riders. The basic
question is that anyone who moves in interstate commerce
should be able to do so freely.

> —*Press conference, Washington,
> D.C., July 19, 1961.*

*The policy of the Kennedys became to encourage the civil rights demon-
strators to channel their energies into registering voters. Robert Kennedy tried to convince civil rights leaders of this in 1961:*

I said that it wasn't as dramatic [as demonstrations]; and
that perhaps there wasn't going to be much publicity. . . . But
I thought that's where they should go and that's what they
should do. I had some conversations with Martin Luther King
along these lines. I think they rather resented it.

> —*Robert F. Kennedy. Interview
> for JFK Oral History,
> December 1964.*

We are confronted primarily with a moral issue. It is as old
as the Scriptures and as plain and as clear as the American
Constitution. The heart of the question is whether all Americans are to be afforded equal rights and equal opportunities.

> —*John F. Kennedy. National
> television address on civil
> rights, June 1963.*

Those of us who are white can only dimly guess at what the pain of racial discrimination must be—what it must be like to be turned away from a public place, or made to use only a segregated portion of that place, for no other reason than the color of one's skin. Prostitutes, criminals, communist and fascist conspirators—these people are free to go to the movies and to choose their own seats, as long as they are white. How can a Negro father explain this intolerable situation to his children? And how can the children be expected to grow up with any sense of pride in being Americans?

>—*Robert F. Kennedy. Address,*
>*Annual Convention of the*
>*Theater Owners of America,*
>*New York City, October 28,*
>*1963.*

There is no question that in the next thirty or forty years a Negro can achieve the position . . . of president of the United States.

>—*Robert F. Kennedy. Voice of*
>*America broadcast, May 26,*
>*1961.*

I'm jealous of the fact that you grew up in a ghetto. I wish I'd had that experience.

>—*Robert F. Kennedy. Remark to*
>*writer Jack Newfield. Quoted*
>*in Jack Newfield,* Robert F.
>Kennedy: A Memoir, *1978.*

If I wasn't a United States senator, I'd rather be working in Bedford-Stuyvesant than any place I know.

>—*Robert F. Kennedy. Remark*
>*after visiting the Brooklyn*
>*ghetto and establishing a*
>*coalition of concerned*
>*businesses to revitalize the*
>*area.*

Stop them! Get your friends off those buses!

> —*John F. Kennedy. Remark on
> the civil rights movement's
> freedom rides to Harris
> Wofford, the administration's
> point man on civil rights.
> According to Wofford, Kennedy
> didn't want to be embarrassed
> before the Soviets at the
> upcoming summit, 1961.*

We live in different worlds and gaze over a different land-scape. Through the eyes of the white majority, the Negro world is one of steady and continuous progress. . . . But if we look through the eyes of a young slum dweller—the Negro, the Puerto Rican, the Mexican-American—there is a different view, and the world is a hopeless place indeed.

> —*Robert F. Kennedy.* To Seek a
> Newer World, *1967.*

When we see society's failures—dropouts or dope addicts, petty thieves or prostitutes—we do not know whether they are Italian or English, Baptist or Orthodox. But we know when they are Negro. So every Negro who fails confirms the voice of prejudice.

> —*Robert F. Kennedy. Speech,
> National Council of Christians
> and Jews, April 28, 1965.*

But the Negro carries his color for life. . . . From birth, he carries an armband that cannot be taken off. If it cannot be taken off, then it must be made a badge of pride and honor. While some use "black power" to preach violence and hate, and thus have made of it a slogan of fear, there are others to whom it means a sense of Negro self-reliance and solidarity, of that group achievement—whether in politics, business, or labor—which has been the base on which earlier minorities achieved full integration into American life.

> —*Robert F. Kennedy.* To Seek a
> Newer World, *1967.*

Like other minority groups, Negroes will bear the major burden of their own progress. They will have to make their own way, as they are doing. But we must remember that other minorities, including my own, also make progress through increasing their political and economic power as well as by individual effort. Nor was that progress completely without violence, fear, and hatred. . . . Nor did other minorities suffer under the special handicaps of the Negro heritage—centuries of slavery and a century of oppression, an intricate web of legal disabilities, and the crushing forces of racial feeling from whose poisons few whites have fully liberated themselves.

—*Robert F. Kennedy. Address,*
University of California at
Berkeley, October 22, 1966.

The army of the resentful and desperate in the North is an army without generals . . . without captains . . . almost without sergeants. . . . Too many Negroes who have succeeded in climbing the ladder of education and well-being have failed to extend their hand to help their fellows on the rungs below. Civil rights leaders cannot with sit-ins change the fact that adults are illiterate. Marches do not create jobs for their children.

—*Robert F. Kennedy. Speech,*
November 3, 1965.

No one has been barred on account of his race from fighting or dying for America—there are no "white" or "colored" signs on the foxholes or graveyards of battle.

—*John F. Kennedy. Message to*
Congress on proposed civil
rights bill, June 19, 1963.

It is pointless to tell Negroes living in northern slums to obey the law. To them, the law is the enemy. . . . The only answer is massive relief with real help going to the young.

—*Robert F. Kennedy. Speech,*
July 1967.

Ultimately we must succeed in wiping out the huge central-city ghettos. By this I do not mean that the outcome will be racial balance in every urban and suburban neighborhood. Many negroes, given a completely free choice, will choose to live in predominantly Negro neighborhoods just as members of other racial and nationality groups have chosen in the past to live predominantly among their own kinsmen. The important thing is that the Negro must have freedom of choice.

> —*Robert F. Kennedy. Address, luncheon of the Federation of Jewish Philanthropies of New York, New York City, January 20, 1966.*

My father was concerned about blacks in one way, and I was concerned about them in another—as people from whom I could get drugs.

> —*David Kennedy. Interview, Peter Collier and David Horowitz, The Kennedys, 1984.*

I don't want to plan or say or write anything until I know which way I want my life to go. But I think whatever I do will probably involve working with blacks.

> —*John F. Kennedy Jr. Remark to family members after returning from South Africa, 1979.*

My father was more concerned with blacks than yours was.

> —*Robert F. Kennedy Jr. In response to John's remark.*

It is not the bigot among us who has brought us to where we are, for men of goodwill ignore him. It is not the racist among us who has brought our society so low, for he is easy to see and discount. We are where we are because all of us are passing through life with our own personal blinders on—we race through the ghetto on expressways looking neither to the right nor the left until we find the comfort of our own home. We favor civil rights bills and feel a warm glow in our hearts when we hear the eloquence of a man like Dr. King. . . . In essence we are all very decent men and women of goodwill, and we are all very busy with our careers and with our families—all too busy . . . to fight injustice, and poverty, and ill will in the immediate world around us.

—*Edward M. Kennedy. Address,*
Jefferson-Jackson Day Dinner,
Denver, August 21, 1968.

Historians of the future will wonder about the years we have just passed through. They will ask how it could be, a century after the Civil War, that black and white had not yet learned to live together in the promise of this land.

—*Edward M. Kennedy. Speech,*
January 26, 1976.

While economic growth is important to all Americans, it is absolutely essential for black Americans. It is the indispensable condition of black progress. Other groups may have achieved a level of comfort for themselves. But they have no right to stop the engines of growth before others have begun to board the train.

—*Edward M. Kennedy. Speech,*
May 7, 1978.

WOMEN

Women compose the majority of voters now. Women not only have political power, they have financial power.

—*John F. Kennedy. Speech to*
League of Catholic Women.
Quoted in the Boston Globe,
November 11, 1945.

Obviously, Miss Craig, not enough.

> —*John F. Kennedy. Response to reporter May Craig when she asked him what he had done for women. Quoted in Morris K. Udall,* Too Funny to Be President, *1988.*

I'm always rather nervous about how you talk about women who are active in politics, whether they want to be talked about as women or as politicians.

> —*John F. Kennedy. To a group of women delegates to the United Nations who had suggested that there might one day be a woman president.*

We left Russia with a vast admiration for the women. They will pave the streets, work in the factories and labor on the farms. But it seems regrettable that they have so little time for any home life or for any real enjoyment of life which, here in America, comes natural to us.

> —*Jean and Pat Kennedy. Article on their visit to the Soviet Union,* Boston Globe, *October 15, 1955.*

He [John Kennedy] said to me a long time ago that one woman is worth ten men. They have the idealism, they have the time to give, and they work without making demands.

> —*Jacqueline Kennedy. Quoted in the* Washington Star, *October 11, 1960.*

It was never expected that I would go into politics or be a lawyer, or have a job, or do any of those things. It was not even dreamed about, talked about, thought of. It wasn't in the realm of possibility. I was lucky to be in a situation after women's liberation that allowed people to dream differently than they would have otherwise been able to.

I'm glad women are working hard in politics, not just giving coffees like Mummy [Ethel Kennedy] used to. None of the girls at school want just to get married. They have a good feeling they can be anything today, not just a teacher or a secretary.

—Kathleen Kennedy Townsend. Interview, quoted in Laurence Leamer, The Kennedy Women, *1994. Kathleen went on to become lieutenant governor of Maryland.*

After two hundred years, I think it is safe to say that women in America are now demanding full equality in every aspect of American life. And after two hundred years, I think they have every right to expect it. Nor can this nation afford to deny it.

—Edward M. Kennedy. Speech, May 18, 1976.

A media representative from an automobile manufacturer told me that the biggest recent change in consumer habits was women getting involved in choosing the family car. Men tended to be brand loyal—once a Buick, always a Buick. Women, on the other hand, tended to be more discriminating and independent-minded. They would test-drive, read reports, and comparison shop.

It cannot be a coincidence that as more and more women vote, we see a corresponding decline in party loyalty and a startling rise in the number of people who call themselves independent.

—John F. Kennedy Jr. Editor's note, George, *September 1996.*

THE DISABLED

Of the two hundred thousand handicapped hired by the federal government since World War II, there is no single record of the employment of a single mentally retarded man or woman.

> —*Eunice Kennedy Shriver.*
> *Statement to the Women's*
> *Committee of the President's*
> *Committee on Employment of*
> *the Handicapped, May 1963.*

I used to think it was something to hide, something not to talk about. But then I learned that almost everyone I know has a relative or good friend who has the problem of a mentally retarded child somewhere in the family. You have no idea how widespread it is. I've won more hats and neckties betting people that they have that problem somewhere among their relatives or good friends.

> —*Joseph P. Kennedy. Interview*
> *in which he first spoke about*
> *his institutionalized daughter,*
> *Rosemary, June 3, 1960.*

Only a decade or so ago, the concept of equal rights for the retarded would not have been taken seriously. The tragedy for the nation is that millions of human beings capable of contributing to society, capable of achieving something that they could be proud of, and capable of individual happiness, were shut away forever.

> —*Edward M. Kennedy. Speech,*
> *October 12, 1976.*

In the rapid pace of society and its emphasis on youth and mobility, the handicapped have been left behind, relegated to the backwaters of society, ostracized by their contemporaries, victimized by unfair attitudes of discrimination.

> —*Edward M. Kennedy. Speech,*
> *June 28, 1978.*

We [Congress] enacted the landmark Americans with Disabilities Act, bringing comprehensive protection for the rights of forty-three million Americans. Because of that law, fellow citizens across the country are finally learning that "disabled" does not mean "unable."

> —Edward M. Kennedy. Remarks
> on Civil Rights, October 22,
> 1993.

HOMOSEXUALITY

Today we seek to take the next step on this journey of justice by banning discrimination based on sexual orientation. . . . We know we cannot change attitudes overnight. But the great lesson of American history is that changes in the law are an essential step in breaking down barriers of bigotry, exposing prejudice for what it is, and building a strong and fair nation.

> —Edward M. Kennedy.
> Statement on the Employment
> Non-Discrimination Act of
> 1995.

Crime and Violence

Crime is not only a cause of economic waste, but far worse than that, it is a reproach to the moral pretensions of our society, and advertises to the world the gap between our pronouncements and our performance.

> —Robert F. Kennedy. Address,
> American Bar Association
> House of Delegates, San
> Francisco, California, August
> 6, 1962.

In 1961, amidst growing concern over violence in movies and on television and its possible contribution to juvenile delinquency, the Senate began an investigation into the issue, with the support of J. Edgar

Hoover, director of the FBI. At a press conference President Kennedy was asked about what he could do about the increasing violence in the media and responded:

This is a matter which goes to the responsibility of the private citizen. The federal government cannot protect the standards of young boys and girls—the parents have to do it in the first place. We can only play a very supplemental role and a marginal role. . . . It rests with the families involved—with the parents involved. But we can do something about the living conditions and the atmosphere in which these children grow up, and we are going to do something about it.

> —*John F. Kennedy. Press conference, February 1, 1961.*

Delinquency is a broad problem and demands a broad attack. Educational programs, job opportunities, recreational facilities, adult counseling—all these projects and many more must be combined in a comprehensive program if we are to make a major impact on the problem. We must show every young person, no matter how deprived his background may be, that he has a genuine opportunity to fulfill himself and play a constructive role in American life. We cannot solve delinquency by building new prisons. We must create new opportunities for our nation's youth.

> —*Robert F. Kennedy, November 1962.*

Crime is going to be a more serious problem in the United States. . . . Violence is an intolerable threat to the future of every American—black or white—to the mind's peace and the body's safety and the community's order—to all that makes life worthwhile.

> —*Robert F. Kennedy. Address, dinner honoring Congressman James C. Corman, Los Angeles, October 21, 1966.*

The more closely one looks at the cost and deployment of our crime prevention efforts, the more apparent it becomes that we have put too much responsibility at the end of the line, rather than at the beginning. Enforcement and correction can do only part of the job.

—*Robert F. Kennedy. Speech,*
1964.

Of all our problems, the most immediate and pressing . . . is the plight of the people of the ghetto, and the violence that has exploded as its product—jumping and spreading across the country, sending fear and anger before it, leaving death and devastation behind. We are now, as we may well be for some time to come, in the midst of what is rapidly becoming the most terrible and urgent domestic crisis to face this nation since the Civil War.

—*Robert F. Kennedy.* To Seek a
Newer World, *1967.*

The riots are not crises that can be resolved as suddenly as they arose. They are a condition that has been with us for 300 years, now worsened and intensified under the strains of modern life.

—*Robert F. Kennedy.* To Seek a
Newer World, *1967.*

We have a responsibility to the victims of crime and violence. It is a responsibility to think not only of our own convenience but of the tragedy of sudden death. It is a responsibility to put away childish things—to make the possession and use of firearms a matter undertaken only by serious people who will use them with the restraint and maturity that their dangerous nature deserves— and demands. For too long we have dealt with these deadly weapons as if they were harmless toys. Yet their very presence, the ease of their acquisition, and the familiarity of their appearance have led to thousands of deaths each year. . . . It is past time that we wipe this stain of violence from our land.

—*Robert F. Kennedy. Speech to*
the first session of the Eighty-
ninth Congress.

It seems as though our country is pulling apart into separate peoples who do not know one another . . . where one group of Americans looks upon another group of Americans with growing mistrust, and even dread. And where, not because we lack the goodwill, but because we lack the faith in ourselves, our response is often to bolt the door, hire more police, and stay as far away from centers of violence as possible.

> *—Edward M. Kennedy. Address, Jefferson-Jackson Day Dinner, Denver, April 5, 1968.*

[We are faced with a type of violence] slower but just as deadly [and] destructive as the gun or the bomb in the night. This is the violence of institutions: indifference and inaction and slow decay. This is the violence that affects the poor, that poisons relations between men because of the color of their skin.

> *—Robert F. Kennedy. Campaign speech, the day after Martin Luther King Jr.'s assassination, 1968.*

We develop the kind of citizens we deserve. If a large number of our children grow up into frustration and poverty, we must expect to pay the price.

> *—Robert F. Kennedy. Address, Young Israel of Pelham Parkway, New York City, May 20, 1964.*

Every society gets the kind of criminal it deserves. What is equally true is that every community gets the kind of law enforcement it insists on.

> *—Robert F. Kennedy. The Pursuit of Justice, 1964.*

National security begins at home. It begins on the streets and sidewalks of our cities. It begins in the small towns and villages of our country. It begins on the farms in our rural areas. These are the places where the first two hundred years of our nation were decided. And these are the places where the fate of America is going to be decided in the third century of our history.

—Edward M. Kennedy. Speech,
March 1, 1976.

The gangsters of today work in a highly organized fashion and are far more powerful now than at any time in the history of the country. They control political figures and threaten whole communities. They have stretched their tentacles of corruption and fear into industries both large and small. They grow stronger every day.

—Robert F. Kennedy. The
Enemy Within, *1960.*

If we do not on a national scale attack organized criminals with weapons and techniques as effective as their own, they will destroy us.

—Robert F. Kennedy. The
Enemy Within, *1960.*

Organized crime is a national problem. The racketeer is not someone dressed in a black shirt, white tie, and diamond stickpin, whose activities affect only a remote underworld circle. He is more likely to be outfitted in a gray flannel suit, and his influence is more likely to be as far-reaching as that of an important industrialist.

—Robert F. Kennedy. Speech,
1964.

When a grown man sat for an evening and talked continually about his toughness, I could only conclude he was a bully hiding behind a facade.

> —*Robert F. Kennedy on his first meeting with Jimmy Hoffa in 1957,* The Enemy Within, *1960.*

I'll jump off the Capitol.

> —*Robert F. Kennedy. Response to a question of what he would do if Hoffa wasn't convicted.*

Told him [Hoffa] I did not want him to talk to our investigators as he had been doing. Told him if he wanted to hate anybody to hate me. He agreed. His eyes were bloodshot. The last two days of hearing he was a beaten man compared to the beginning. His tone was subdued and no longer did he give the hate looks that he enjoyed so much in the beginning.

> —*Robert F. Kennedy. Journal entry, 1957.*

My first love is Hoffa.

> —*Robert F. Kennedy. Interview with the* Saturday Evening Post, *June 8, 1959.*

They are sleek, often bilious and fat, or lean and cold and hard. They have the smooth faces and cold eyes of gangsters. They wore the same rich clothes, the diamond ring, the jeweled watch, the strong, sickly-sweet smelling perfume.

> —*Robert F. Kennedy on the witnesses that appeared at the second round of hearings involving Hoffa,* The Enemy Within, *1960.*

Based on some estimates, guns are statistically like rats. They outnumber our population. Not surprisingly, our output of ammunition for civilian firearms almost staggers the imagination. American industry outdoes all other nations in the production of bullets. Nearly five billion rounds of ammunition flow through the marketplace each year. . . . All of those bullets could not only wipe out the world's entire human population, but destroy much of the world's wildlife as well.

—*Edward M. Kennedy. Address, Businessmen's Executive Movement for Peace in Vietnam, February 17, 1971.*

Families like mine all across this country know all too well what the damage of weapons can do. And you want to arm our people even more. . . . Shame on you! What in the world are you thinking when you're opening up the debate on this issue. . . ? You'll never know, Mr. Chairman, what it's like. Because you don't have someone in your family who was killed. It's not the person killed, it's the whole family that's affected.

Furthermore, people will say, and I've heard this argument already, that this [the assault weapon ban] is not effective because it's not cutting crime. That is the wrong question. It's not about cutting crime, it's about cutting the number of people who get killed by these assault weapons. You're asking the wrong question. It's not about crime. That's what we're advocating in proposing this ban, and that's why we should keep this ban in place.

—*Patrick J. Kennedy. House floor speech, March 1996.*

Civil Disobedience and Dissent

I want every American to stand up for their rights, even if he has to sit down for them.

—*John F. Kennedy. Campaign speech on the sit-in at southern lunch counters, August 3, 1960.*

Americans are free . . . to disagree with the law, but not to disobey it.

—*John F. Kennedy. Speech, September 30, 1962.*

Those who make peaceful revolution impossible will make violent revolution inevitable.

—*John F. Kennedy. Speech, March 13, 1962.*

The fires of discord are busy in every city. Redress is sought in the street, in demonstrations, parades, and protests which create tensions and threaten violence. We face, therefore, a moral crisis as a country and as a people.

—*John F. Kennedy. National television address, June 11, 1963.*

There will always be dissident voices heard in the land, expressing opposition without alternative, finding fault but never favor, perceiving gloom on every side and seeking influence without responsibility. Those voices are inevitable.

—*John F. Kennedy. Undelivered speech, Dallas, Texas, November 22, 1963.*

Those who advocate disobedience of our laws, following their thoughts to the ultimate, are advocating that we change our form of government.

> —*Robert F. Kennedy. Speech, Conference of UPI Editors and Publishers, Washington, D.C., June 7, 1961.*

Protest for redress of just grievances is the right and the duty of every citizen in a free society. But protest must not be allowed to distract our attention from the job at hand—nor may the need of protest be used as an excuse for our own inaction.

> —*Robert F. Kennedy. Address, Borough Presidents Conference of Community Leaders, January 21, 1966.*

It is not enough to allow dissent. We must demand it. For there is much to dissent from. . . .

Yet we must, as thinking men, distinguish between the right of dissent and the way we choose to exercise that right. It is not enough to justify or explain our actions by the fact that they are legal or constitutionally protected. The Constitution protects wisdom and ignorance, compassion and selfishness alike. That dissent which consists simply of sporadic and dramatic acts sustained by neither continuing labor or research—that dissent which seeks to demolish while lacking both the desire and direction for rebuilding, that dissent which, contemptuously or out of laziness, casts aside the practical weapons and instruments of change and progress—that kind of dissent is merely self-indulgence.

> —*Robert F. Kennedy. Speech to students, University of California at Berkeley, October 22, 1966.*

If I hadn't been born rich, I'd probably be a revolutionary.

> —Robert F. Kennedy to English
> journalist Margaret Laing.
> Quoted in Laing, Robert
> Kennedy, 1968.

Our turmoil was dramatized all too well by a news photograph showing a construction worker in New Jersey beating up a student holding an unfamiliar flag. As it turned out, the student was a conservative young man who supported the extension of the war, and the flag was that of his college fraternity. But that did not matter. He was young. He was carrying a flag. And so he was someone to be against, to prejudice, to assault, to curse. And on the other hand we have seen students committing unthinkable verbal violence, calling police officers "pigs" without even knowing what they think, or who they are, or how they feel toward public issues.

> —Edward M. Kennedy.
> Commencement address,
> Manhattanville College, May
> 30, 1970.

There are many who criticize youth for not being more obedient to our traditions. What they fail to understand is that the questions of our youth are disturbing because they are questions we ourselves find hard to answer. They are questions we ourselves refuse to face.

> —Edward M. Kennedy. Speech,
> First National Regional
> Conference of the National
> Council for Social Studies,
> April 11, 1970.

No longer is it possible to dismiss a campus disturbance as a manifestation of unique local factors. . . . A common thread runs from campus to campus, whose dominant feature is the apparent collision between the irresistible force of youth and the immovable object of faceless and unresponsive institutions at all levels—federal and local, public and private, business and academic.

> —*Edward M. Kennedy.*
> *Testimony before the*
> *Commission on Campus*
> *Unrest, Washington, D.C.,*
> *July 15, 1970.*

Dissent, like so many other things in the America of 1970, has become too comfortable. It takes five minutes to draw the letters on a protest sign, but it takes a lifetime of dedicated service to make a contribution to society.

> —*Edward M. Kennedy.*
> *Distinguished Lecture Series,*
> *Boston University, September*
> *15, 1970.*

"A Nation of Immigrants"

Our attitude toward immigration reflects our faith in the American ideal. We have always believed it possible for men and women who start at the bottom to rise as far as their talent and energy allow. Neither race nor place of birth should affect their chances.

> —*Robert F. Kennedy.*
> *Introduction to 1964 edition*
> *of* A Nation of Immigrants, *by*
> *John F. Kennedy.*

I was born in this country! My children were born in this country! What the hell does someone have to do to become an American?

> —*Joseph P. Kennedy. Response*
> *when a Boston newspaper*
> *referred to him as an*
> *"Irishman," c. 1930.*

Those narrow-minded bigoted sons of bitches barred me because I was an Irish Catholic and son of a barkeep.

> —*Joseph P. Kennedy. Remark after his application for membership in the Cohasset Country Club was rejected, c. 1925.*

Well, Rose . . . this is a helluva long way from East Boston.

> —*Joseph P. Kennedy. Remark while preparing for dinner with the king and queen of England, 1937.*

The influence of Irish culture in this country must be recognized as on the wane. Nor is it likely that anything or any person can change this process of cultural absorption.

> —*Joseph P. Kennedy. Speech, Clover Club, March 13, 1937.*

Tell me, when *will* the nice people of Boston accept us?

> —*Rose Kennedy. Remark to a friend while John F. Kennedy was attending Harvard.*

Do you know it is impossible for an Irish Catholic to get into the Somerset Club in Boston? If I moved back to Boston even after being president, it would make no difference.

> —*John F. Kennedy. Remark to a friend, June 1963.*

Just remember that this country is not a private preserve for Protestants. There's a whole new generation out there and it's filled with the sons and daughters of immigrants from all over the world, and those people are going to be mighty proud that one of their own is running for president. And that pride will be your spur, it will give your campaign an intensity we've never seen in public life. Mark my word, I know it's true.

> —*Joseph P. Kennedy. Remark to John F. Kennedy, planning the 1960 presidential bid, 1956.*

When my great-grandfather left here to become a cooper in East Boston, he carried nothing with him except a strong religious faith and a strong desire for liberty. If he hadn't left, I would be working at the Albatross Company across the road.

> —*John F. Kennedy. Speech, Ireland, 1963.*

The outpouring of love was really ovewhelming. I mean, it's very exciting to have somebody leave Ireland and have their descendant, the president of the United States, one hundred years later come back to visit. It's really tear time. And he was so great, you know, responding to everybody. And he was so thrilled himself. He was just thrilled how they responded. I never saw him so excited. Oh, yeah. It was so touching, such a poetic experience.

> —*Jean Kennedy Smith. Comments on her 1963 trip to Ireland with John and Eunice.*

In part to be an American means to have been an outcast and a stranger, to have come to the exiles' country, and to know that he who denies the outcast and stranger still amongst us, he also denies America.

> —*Robert F. Kennedy. Speech, Citizens Union, New York City, December 14, 1967.*

It is my conviction that there are few areas in our law which more urgently demand reform than our present unfair system of choosing the immigrants we will allow to enter the United States. It is a source of embarrassment to us around the world. It is a source of loss to the economic and creative strength of our nation as a whole.

> —*Robert F. Kennedy. Speech, 1964.*

It is a source of anguish to many of our own citizens with relatives from abroad. . . . Under the law, an American citizen born in one country can get a maid or gardener from another country but must wait a year or more to be united with his mother.

—*Robert F. Kennedy. Speech,*
1965.

The melting pot of America has made the whole of our nation greater than the sum of its parts.

—*Edward M. Kennedy. Speech,*
October 12, 1970.

As citizens of the world's oldest republic, whose sons "fired the shot heard around the world," we cannot be deaf to the voices of other people straining to be heard, of people struggling to share in freedom. And once we learn this lesson, America will again be a symbol of hope and freedom for people in other lands.

—*Edward M. Kennedy. Speech,*
May 1, 1975.

The Irish yield to none in their role in the making of America. They have left their mark in every facet of American life. Wherever we look, in business and the labor movement, in literature and music and sports, in science and religion, in public service at every level of government, we find citizens of Irish descent who built our nation and helped to make it strong.

—*Edward M. Kennedy. Speech,*
May 18, 1977.

Let's reject the naysayers who say that America is no longer big enough for the parents, the children, and the brothers and sisters of our own citizens—no longer big enough to be a haven for refugees fleeing persecution. Sensible reform, yes. Slam the door, no. Immigrants have always helped make the America of tomorrow even greater than the America of today, and they always will. It's part of what makes America America. Let's not abandon it. Let's honor our ideals, not reject them.

> —Edward M. Kennedy. Remarks
> on the Immigration Reform
> Act of 1996, which would
> severely limit families of legal
> immigrants from joining their
> relatives in the U.S., February
> 29, 1996.

The Media

I not only could not stifle controversy among your readers— I welcome it. This administration intends to be candid about its errors; for, as a wise man once said: "An error doesn't become a mistake until you refuse to correct it." We intend to accept full responsibility for our errors; and we expect you to point them out when we miss them.

> —John F. Kennedy. Speech,
> American Newspaper
> Publishers Association, New
> York City, April 27, 1961.

Maybe if you had printed more about the [Bay of Pigs] operation, you would have saved us from a colossal mistake.

> —John F. Kennedy.
> Conversation with the New
> York Times managing editor,
> Turner Catledge, April 1961.

During the 1960 campaign, John F. Kennedy felt it necessary to make a plea to the press about the "religious issue":

The members of the press should report the facts as they find them. They should describe the issues as they see them. But they should beware, it seems to me, of either magnifying this issue or oversimplifying it.

One article, for example, supposedly summing the Wisconsin primary up in advance, mentioned the word "Catholic" twenty times in fifteen paragraphs—not mentioning even once dairy farms, disarmament, labor legislation, or any other issue. And on the Sunday before the primary, the *Milwaukee Journal* featured a map of the state, listing county by county the relative strength of three types of voters—Democrats, Republicans, and Catholics.

> —*John F. Kennedy. Speech, American Society of Newspaper Editors, Washington, D.C., April 21, 1960.*

Asked in a press conference how he saw the news media now that he was president, Kennedy replied:

Well, I am reading more and enjoying it less . . . but I have not complained, nor do I plan to make any general complaints. I read and talk to myself about it, but I don't plan to issue any general statement on the press. I think that they are doing their task, as a critical branch, the fourth estate. And I am attempting to do mine. And we are going to live together for a period, and then go our separate ways.

> —*John F. Kennedy. News conference, Washington, D.C., May 9, 1962.*

The press can resist the standard of the lowest common denominator, the rationalization that all news is fit to print that has appeared anywhere else.

> —*Edward Kennedy.*

The president has said: "Ask not what your country can do for you—ask what you can do for your country." And many writers have said: "Tell us, Mr. President, tell the American people and they will do it."

I think myself that if we have to be told, we are in a bad way.

—Robert F. Kennedy. Speech, Joint Defense Appeal of the American Jewish Committee and the Anti-Defamation League of B'nai B'rith, Chicago, June 21, 1961.

I would say that it [the news media] is an invaluable arm of the presidency, as a check really on what is going on in the administration, and more things come to my attention that cause me concern or give me information. So I would think that Mr. Khrushchev, operating a totalitarian system—which has many "advantages" as far as being able to move in secret, and all the rest—there is a terrific disadvantage in not having the abrasive quality of the press applied to you daily. . . . Even though we never liked it, and even though we wish they didn't write it, and even though we disapprove, there isn't any doubt that we could not do the job at all in a free society without a very, very active press.

—John F. Kennedy. Television and radio interview, "Year-end Conversation with the President," Washington, D.C., December 17, 1962.

If there's more than one person—including yourself—in a room, consider anything said to be on the record and a probable headline in the morning paper.

—John F. Kennedy. Quoted in Time, *February 6, 1989.*

I do not believe that newspapermen are self-appointed judges of what's right and wrong, or what's good and bad. But I believe in and greatly admire those who are competent to see the truth and inform the people. In my opinion, the newspapers are equal to the courts—and sometimes ahead of the courts, in our system—in protecting the people's fundamental rights.

> —Robert F. Kennedy. Speech,
> annual luncheon of the
> Associated Press, New York,
> April 23, 1962.

I think it is very clear that a newspaper can be a major difference in whether an issue is going to be settled in the courts—or in the streets.

> —Robert F. Kennedy. Speech,
> Conference of UPI Editors and
> Publishers, Washington, D.C.,
> June 7, 1961.

The great recent social and political conflicts in our own generation—the civil rights movement, the struggle to end the war in Vietnam, the response to Watergate—depended for their success on a free press and the exercise of free speech. What we were, what we are, and what we shall be as a nation and as individuals are closely bound up with that single, simple phrase "Congress shall make no law abridging the freedom of speech."

> —Edward M. Kennedy. Speech,
> June 13, 1978.

I think that people must be as sick of hearing about us . . . as I am.

> —Jacqueline Kennedy. Quoted in
> Ladies Home Journal, October
> 1962.

I get afraid of reporters when they come to me in a crowd. I don't like crowds because I don't like impersonal masses. They remind me of swarms of locusts.

The truth of the matter is that I am a very shy person. People take my diffidence for arrogance and my withdrawal from publicity as a sign, supposedly, that I am looking down on the rest of mankind.

> —*Jacqueline Kennedy Onassis.*
> *Interview,* Kayham
> International, *Tehran, Iran,*
> *May 25, 1972.*

Business and Economy

THE KENNEDY FORTUNE

Big businessmen are the most overrated men in the country. Here I am, a boy from East Boston, and I took 'em. So don't be impressed.

> —*Joseph P. Kennedy. Remark,*
> *1929.*

It's easy to make money in the market. We'd better get in before they pass a law against it.

> —*Joseph P. Kennedy. Comment*
> *on the stock market, c. 1922.*

Never meet anybody after two for lunch. Meet in the morning because you're sharper. Never have long lunches. They're not only boring, but dangerous because of the martinis.

> —*Joseph P. Kennedy's*
> *philosophy of business*
> *meetings.*

I did so poorly in a course in banking and finance that I had to drop out after the first semester.

> —*Joseph P. Kennedy. Interview*
> *with* Fortune, *which had just*
> *estimated his wealth at $250*
> *million, 1957.*

Why didn't you tell me that we had all that money?

> —*Rose Kennedy. Remark to Joseph Kennedy after* Fortune *estimated his worth at $250 million, 1957.*

Only a fool holds out for the top dollar.

> —*Joseph P. Kennedy. Remark on how to win on Wall Street.*

We must get into the picture business. This is a new industry and a gold mine. In fact, it looks like another telephone industry.

> —*Joseph P. Kennedy on the motion picture industry, c. 1925.*

When you make a steel rail, you make something that is so long and heavy and of such a quality. But when you make a foot of film, it is subject to the judgment of millions of people, each with his own standard of measurement.

> —*Joseph P. Kennedy. Interview, the* New York Times, *June 3, 1928.*

Take Boston. The Cabots and the Lodges wouldn't be caught dead at pictures, or let their children go. And that's why their servants know more about what's going on than they do. The working class gets smarter every day, thanks to radio and pictures. It's the snooty Back Bay bankers who are missing the boat.

> —*Joseph P. Kennedy. Remark to actress Gloria Swanson on why banks were slow to invest in Hollywood, 1927.*

What this corporation needs, first and most of all, is a box of Havana cigars.

> —*Joseph P. Kennedy. Remark*
> *upon taking his seat as*
> *president of Film Booking*
> *Office of America, 1926.*

My father built his financial empire with a secretary and a telephone.

> —*Eunice Kennedy Shriver.*

If you want to make money, go where the money is.

> —*Joseph P. Kennedy. Remark*
> *on his relocation to New York*
> *in 1926.*

I am not ashamed to record that in those days I felt and said I would be willing to part with half of what I had if I could be sure of keeping, under law and order, the other half. Then it seemed that I should be able to hold nothing for the protection of my family.

> —*Joseph P. Kennedy.* I'm for
> Roosevelt, *1936, on his mood*
> *during the Great Depression.*

I have yet to be indebted to anybody in Wall Street.

> —*Joseph P. Kennedy. Remark*
> *shortly after becoming first*
> *chairman of the Securities*
> *Exchange Commission.*

I have never discussed money with my wife and family, and I never will.

> —*Joseph P. Kennedy. Quoted in*
> *James Burns,* John Kennedy:
> A Political Profile, *1960.*

I fixed it so that any of my children, financially speaking, could look me in the eye and tell me to go to hell.

> —*Joseph P. Kennedy. Boasting to friends about his children's trust funds.*

My father used his money to free us—not to hold us.

> —*Robert F. Kennedy. Remark to a friend.*

I really began to make money when I came down here to sit on my butt and think.

> —*Joseph P. Kennedy. Remark to a friend after he began to work out of his Palm Beach residence, using long-distance calls to make deals from poolside.*

ECONOMICS

Economic prophecy is at best an uncertain art—as demonstrated by [my] prediction one year ago from this same podium that 1960 would be, and I quote, "the most prosperous year in our history."

> —*John F. Kennedy. State of the Union Address, January 30, 1961.*

What is at stake in our economic decisions today is not some grand warfare of rival ideologies which will sweep the country with passion but the practical management of a modern economy. What we need is not labels and clichés but more basic discussion of the sophisticated and technical questions involved in keeping a great economic machinery moving ahead.

The national interest lies in high employment and steady expansion of output, in stable prices and a strong dollar. The declaration of such objectives is easy; their attainment in an intricate and interdependent economy and world is a little more difficult. To attain them, we require not some automatic response but hard thought.

> —*John F. Kennedy.*
> *Commencement address, Yale*
> *University, New Haven,*
> *Connecticut, June 11, 1962.*

Inflation is a serious problem. Its solution is going to strain our most enlightened economists and policy makers. But let us get on with the job of finding the right remedies for inflation, without resorting to the time-dishonored tactic of ravaging the economy in the process. If we learn anything from our present troubles, let it be the lesson that this is the last time the nation has to suffer because of the dangerous myth that a scorched-earth policy of recession is the answer to inflation.

> —*Edward M. Kennedy. Speech,*
> *March 12, 1975.*

This nation cannot allow its economy to drift toward the future as though 10 or 15 percent inflation were the natural order of the American economic universe.

> —*Edward M. Kennedy. Speech,*
> *June 14, 1979.*

Economists tell us that NAFTA will mean a net gain in jobs in the years ahead. . . . But what is causing so much difficulty is the little word with big implications—"net." That word slips easily off economists' tongues. But it has a devastating impact on all those who are caught in the "net" and whose jobs and livelihoods are at risk.

> —*Edward M. Kennedy.*
> *Statement on the North*
> *American Free Trade*
> *Agreement, November 20,*
> *1993.*

CAPITALISM IN AMERICA

We are now on the eve of big consolidations. They have become practically necessary. . . . Ours is an industry that lends itself very easily to consolidation.

—*Joseph P. Kennedy. Answering*
a question about the future of
the motion picture industry at
his Harvard lecture series,
1927.

An organized functioning society requires a planned economy. The more complex the society the greater the demand for planning. Otherwise there results a haphazard and inefficient method of social control, and in the absence of planning the law of the jungle prevails. . . . [Mass unemployment is] the Achilles heel of freedom . . . the root of all the ills and ailments of subjugated people in Europe. . . . Planned action is imperative, or else capitalism and the American scheme of life will be in serious jeopardy.

—*Joseph P. Kennedy.* I'm for
Roosevelt, *1936.*

On the state of mind of the American businessman faced with the
New Deal:

His *moral* prestige is gone. . . . He is being judged by new standards which are quite unfamiliar to him. He feels exposed. He has been shaken in his own faith in himself. He is made to doubt secretly that he represents the American system in its most perfect expression. All this is unconscious and all the more frightful. Being unable—and certainly unwilling—to analyze with coolness the cause of anxiety, he seeks relief in vituperation and hatred.

—*Joseph P. Kennedy. Radio*
speech, October 21, 1936.

For month after month the country was treated to a series of amazing revelations which involved practically all the important names in the financial community in practices which, to say the least, were highly unethical. The belief that those in control of the corporate life of America were motivated by honesty and ideals of honorable conduct was completely shattered.

—Joseph P. Kennedy. On the 1932 hearings of the Senate Banking and Currency Committee, I'm for Roosevelt, 1936.

[Short-term traders, or "bears," perform] a useful function when they don't carry their policy to extremes. . . . Really, it takes more courage and cunning to be a bear than to be a bull. A bear is betting against the popular, optimistic side of business sentiment.

—Joseph P. Kennedy. Remark while chairman of the SEC.

I wish I hadn't acquired respectability. I'd be out selling the market short.

—Joseph P. Kennedy. Speech, Economic Club of Chicago, 1945.

In 1937 Joseph Kennedy was appointed to the chair of a commission to bring into effect new laws governing the vitally important and horribly administrated merchant marine. After meeting with a group of ship owners, he remarked to his colleague John Burns:

KENNEDY: Now you can see why the merchant marine is in lousy shape.

BURNS: What's wrong?

KENNEDY: Why, there wasn't a guy in that room who could write a check for a million dollars.

Whether we keep our free economy or trade it for something about which we know very little is the big political issue ahead. It is up to businessmen to sell our economic system to the public. They must do as good a job on that as they do on their own products. Unless the advantages of our system over others are brought home to everyone, there is no reason to believe that the trend toward more and more government will be checked.

—Joseph P. Kennedy. Speech,
Chicago Economic Club,
December 1945.

In 1945 Chairman of the British Labour Party Harold Laski stated that capitalism was dead in America, and that America should become socialist to survive. This statement caused Joseph Kennedy to reply:

How can Laski have the gall to assert that capitalism is dead when the British Empire has been twice saved in thirty years by the capitalistic United States? I know Laski and he is an arrogant apostle of anarchy who has spent his time shuttling between Moscow, London and New Haven peddling his particular brand of socialism.

—Quoted in the Chicago Daily
Tribune, *December 6, 1945.*

On April 10, 1962, United States Steel Corporation announced that they would raise the price of steel by six dollars a ton. The corporation had just reached an agreement with the United Steel Workers of America that granted a wage increase and ruled out a price increase. President Kennedy, enraged, recalled advice from his father's life in business:

My father always told me that all businessmen were sons of bitches, but I never believed it until now.

They fucked us and we've got to try to fuck them.

—John F. Kennedy. Remark on
U.S. Steel, April 13, 1962.

If they [steel magnates] don't do well, I don't do well.
>—*John F. Kennedy. Quoted in*
>Time, *November 7, 1988.*

Our enemies assert that capitalism enslaves the worker and will destroy itself. It is our national faith that the system of competitive enterprise offers the best hope for individual freedom, social development, and economic growth. Thus, every businessman who cheats on his taxes, fixes prices, or underpays his labor, every union official who makes a collusive deal, misuses union funds, damages the free enterprise system in the eyes of the world and does a disservice to the millions of honest Americans in all walks of life.
>—*Robert F. Kennedy. Speech,*
>*Law Day exercises, University*
>*of Georgia Law School, May*
>*6, 1961.*

In a survey last year, only 12 percent of all graduating college seniors hoped for a career in business, or thought such a career would be worthwhile and satisfying. Why? Part of the answer, surely, is that the great corporations which are so large a part of the American life play so small a role in the solution of its problems.
>—*Robert F. Kennedy. Address,*
>*Americans for Democratic*
>*Action dinner, Philadelphia,*
>*February 24, 1967.*

Private enterprise is not just another part of America; in a significant sense, it is the very sinew and strength of America.
>—*Robert F. Kennedy.* To Seek a
>Newer World, *1967.*

A sound economy is the greatest social program America ever had, the source of our hopes for action on all the other issues facing us.
>—*Edward M. Kennedy. Speech,*
>*April 2, 1976.*

A weak American economy poses the greatest threat today to international American stability. So long as the economy is wrong, nothing else is right.

—*Edward M. Kennedy. Speech,*
January 21, 1977.

The sad fact is that today small companies and private citizens are Davids without slingshots, competing against corporate and governmental Goliaths in wars of attrition which have become increasingly difficult to win.

The American people are not just concerned about "big government"; they are also concerned about the control exerted by "big business."

—*Edward M. Kennedy. Speech,*
August 7, 1978.

The heart and soul of our economy is small businesses. They are the people who hire the vast majority of American people. They are the ones with the entrepreneurial dreams and goals who get out and get something done. I don't care if you are a pizza-parlor owner or a doughnut-shop owner or a cobbler. The closer we can get banks to provide home mortgage loans to those folks, the better off the country is going to be.

—*Joseph P. Kennedy II.*
Remarks on the Home
Mortgage Disclosure Act.
Quoted in the Boston Globe
Magazine, *May 23, 1993.*

UNEMPLOYMENT

When you have 7 percent unemployed, you have 93 percent working.

—*John F. Kennedy. Quoted in*
Barbara Rowes, The Book of
Quotes, *1979.*

The question is whether we can maintain a reasonable balance between increase in purchasing power and the cost of doing business with full employment. That is the basic problem. I'm not satisfied to have the cost of living remain constant only by having the economy restrained.

> —*John F. Kennedy. Response to the question of whether there was any danger of inflation, press conference, February 1, 1961.*

Unemployment is bad enough when there's a recession, but it is intolerable when there is prosperity.

> —*John F. Kennedy. Press conference, Washington, D.C., July 19, 1961.*

Have you ever told a coal miner in West Virginia or Kentucky that what he needs is individual initiative to go out and get a job where there isn't any?

> —*Robert F. Kennedy, August 1964.*

BUSINESS AND GOVERNMENT

The days of stock manipulation are in the past now. There will be little, if any, of this "buy today and out Thursday" business from this time on. Times have changed and things that seemed all right four or five years ago are now out of the picture.

> —*Joseph P. Kennedy. Remarks to reporters on his first day as Chairman of the SEC, quoted in the* New York Times, *July 4, 1934.*

Everybody says that what business needs is confidence. I agree. Confidence that if business does the right thing, it will be protected and given a chance to live, make profits and grow, helping itself and helping the country. . . . [We are not] coroners sitting on the corpse of financial enterprise. There are no grudges to satisfy, no venom which needs victims. The rules are simple and honest. Only those who see things crookedly will find them harsh.

> —*Joseph P. Kennedy. Speech on the role of the SEC, National Press Club, July 25, 1934.*

Don't dodge the duties of citizenship by blaming government . . . for the lack of business initiative and enterprise.

> —*Joseph P. Kennedy. Address at a luncheon attended by one thousand businessmen. Quoted in the New York Times, March 20, 1935.*

I had a hunch that this boy was trying to razzle-dazzle us into giving him something for nothing. So I called him in, told him his claim wasn't worth a cent, and we'd fight any suit he brought for any amount; and when he swallowed that and settled for nothing, then I *knew* he'd been trying to razzle-dazzle us.

> —*Joseph P. Kennedy. Interview on his dealings with the merchant marine on behalf of the federal government, Fortune, September 1937. His five-man commission settled $73 million of claims of twenty-three companies for less than $750,000 in seventy-three days.*

It would be premature to ask your support in the next election, and it would be inaccurate to thank you for it in the past.

> —*John F. Kennedy. Remark to a group of businessmen soon after his election, 1961.*

At a presidential news conference during a stock market slump:

REPORTER: One reputable columnist after talking to businessmen, obviously, reported this week their attitude is now, we have you where we want you. Have you seen any reflection of this attitude?

JOHN F. KENNEDY: I can't believe I'm where business—big business—wants me.

The talent for getting money out of the Treasury is not the talent that makes a business go.

> —*John P. Kennedy. Remark on subsidies, the* New York Times, *May 23, 1937.*

The pendulum has now swung, so you are entirely in the hands of government when it comes to finance. You can know trends and the principles of the stock market, you can work out charts and tables, and in five minutes someone in Washington can knock you into a cocked hat.

> —*Joseph P. Kennedy. Speech, Boston Latin School Association, 1952.*

One of the business journals took a poll among five hundred businessmen on who they favored for president. I got one vote and I understand they are looking for him.

> —*Robert F. Kennedy. Campaign speech before several hundred prominent businessmen, Portland, Oregon, 1968.*

I'm the only candidate opposed by both big business *and* big labor.

> —*Robert F. Kennedy, 1968.*

Economic growth and productivity and material well-being are the handmaidens of liberty.

> —*John F. Kennedy. Press luncheon, Paris, France, June 2, 1961.*

I look upon the antitrust laws as being "probusiness." I believe firmly that the purpose of the antitrust laws is to protect and promote the competitive interests of business, small and large, as well as to protect the public.

> —*Robert F. Kennedy. Speech, 1964.*

Cars can be made more safe, but automobile manufacturers have not done so. . . . The industry has claimed that the problems of brake failure, tire collapse, and other major failures are beyond engineering skill. These same manufacturers are willing to guarantee the reliability of complex missile and space systems they sell to the armed forces. The contrast is odd indeed. I submit that there is no lack of engineering ability in the United States today. The truth is that engineers are not asked to design for safety.

> —*Robert F. Kennedy. Speech, American Trial Lawyers Association, 1966.*

Regulators all too often encourage or approve unreasonably high prices, inadequate service, and anticompetitive behavior. The cost of this regulation is always passed on to the consumer. And that cost is astronomical.

> —*Edward M. Kennedy. Senate hearings, 1975.*

One of the basic assumptions of our political system is that large centers of unaccountable power are inconsistent with democratic government and the values of a free society. If there is a single theme that ties together the best in both liberal and conservative political traditions, it is this hostility to unchecked power. If the awesome power of giant corporations is no longer adequately checked by the discipline of the market, it is not just our pocketbook that is in jeopardy, it is our liberty.

—Edward M. Kennedy. Speech,
May 3, 1977.

I regard competition as the cornerstone of our free-enterprise system. Along with the Bill of Rights, it is the most important distinguishing feature of our nation in the world community, a beacon for many other nations who are striving to emulate our two-hundred-year-old example of freedom and prosperity. . . .

We should wear the chip of competition on our shoulder, and we should dare the regulators to knock it off.

—Edward M. Kennedy. Speech,
June 30, 1977.

FARMING

The real wealth of a nation resides in its farms and factories and the people who man them.

—John F. Kennedy. Quoted in
Susan Teltser-Schwartz,
Money Talks, *1988.*

The American farmer is the only man in our economy who buys everything he buys at retail, sells everything he sells at wholesale, and pays the freight both ways.

—John F. Kennedy. Campaign
speech, Des Moines, Iowa,
September 22, 1960.

Justice is land for those who live by farming—and all the world has seen that free farmers on their own land are the surest means to an abundant agriculture.

> —*Robert F. Kennedy. Statement to Peruvian students, November 1965.*

We all understand the vital role the farmer plays in our economy and around the world; yet it is incredible to me that this great country cannot develop a farm policy that guarantees an adequate supply of food for every citizen and a fair return for every farmer. . . . America's national pie is big enough for all of us to share.

> —*Edward M. Kennedy, May 26, 1976.*

Labor and Unions

[We are] reaping the whirlwind of a quarter century mishandling of labor relations. We complain about the lack of responsibility of labor and for years we did our best to render labor organizations impotent.

> —*Joseph P. Kennedy. Speech, twenty-fifth class reunion, Harvard class of 1912, 1937.*

Between birth and burial, the Teamsters drive the trucks that clothe and feed and provide the vital necessities of life. They control the pickup and deliveries of milk, frozen meat, fresh fruit, department store merchandise, newspapers, railroad express, air freight, and of cargo to and from the sea docks. Quite literally your life—the life of every person in the United States—is in the hands of Hoffa and his Teamsters.

> —*Robert F. Kennedy. Closing statements in case against Hoffa before the Senate Rackets Committee, 1959.*

The history of this nation rests on the skills of its workers no less than it does on the achievements of its scholars.

> —*Edward M. Kennedy. Speech,*
> *October 19, 1975.*

The building trades [unions] met in Washington and sent an emissary to Jack telling him that he shouldn't appoint me [attorney general] as they would consider it with disfavor. This was one of the motivating forces in my taking the job.

> —*Robert F. Kennedy.*
> *Memorandum, February 8,*
> *1961.*

For all their hard work and successful efforts in the building of America, the blue-collar workers of this country asked little in return. They did not ask for leisure or luxury. They did not ask for free rides or special privileges. They did not ask for subsidized martinis in their lunch pails. They asked only a fair chance to practice their trade; a fair chance to support their families; a fair chance to make their way in life without unwarranted intrusion by their management or their government.

> —*Edward M. Kennedy. Speech,*
> *April 23, 1979.*

This is a basic American struggle.

> —*Robert F. Kennedy. Speech to*
> *the United Farm Workers,*
> *then involved in a strike with*
> *growers in Kern County,*
> *California, 1966.*

The "Quiet Depression" facing American workers is the central economic, social, and political issue of 1996. When the economy is wrong, nothing else is right. Progress and opportunity for all is a fundamental American value. We know the problem. We know its urgency. The only thing that is unacceptable is to do nothing.

Americans are working harder and earning less. Their standard of living is stagnant or sinking. They are worried about losing their jobs, losing their health insurance, affording their children's education, caring for their elderly parents, and somehow still saving for their own retirement. The rich are still getting richer, but more and more families are left out and left behind. The rising tide that once lifted all the boats now lifts only the yachts.

> —*Edward M. Kennedy.*
> *Statement regarding*
> *introduction of The American*
> *Workers Economic Security*
> *Act. Quoted in* Roll Call,
> *March 25, 1996.*

When your children and grandchildren take their place in America—going to high school, and college, and taking good jobs at good pay—when you look at them, you will say, "I did this. I was there, at the point of difficulty and danger." And though you may be old and bent from many years of labor, no man will stand taller than you when you say, "I marched with Cesar [Chávez, leader of the United Farm Workers]."

> —*Robert F. Kennedy. Speech to*
> *members of the UFW*
> *following the Mass of*
> *Thanksgiving, March 10,*
> *1968.*

As a nation, we are moving farther and farther away from the concept that work should pay, that full-time, year-round workers should be able to keep their families out of poverty. . . . There is an old saying that "the rich get richer and the poor get poorer." But that should not be our national economic policy. . . . Now is the time to make the minimum wage a fair wage.

> —Edward M. Kennedy.
> Statement on Amendment to
> Raise the Minimum Wage,
> March 26, 1996.

I know I couldn't get by on $1.50 an hour, and I doubt Mr. Rockefeller could.

> —Robert F. Kennedy. Remark
> on New York Republican
> Governor Nelson Rockefeller,
> who opposed a state bill to
> raise the minimum wage to
> $1.50 per hour.

This issue presents a stark choice about who we represent here in the Senate. "Which side are we on?" Are we on the side of the workers and retirees who struggle to find some economic security in their old age, or the side of wheeler-dealers, corporate raiders, and the super rich?

> —Edward M. Kennedy. Statement
> on pension plan reversions,
> November 11, 1995.

Certainly the free market and the states have a role to play in establishing a framework for job training. But so does the federal government. All three components are important. The metaphor of the three-legged stool applies. If you saw off one leg, the whole stool falls over. . . .

America cannot successfully compete with newly industrializing nations on the basis of which country can pay the lowest wages. It's a mistake to even try. It makes no sense to run a race to the bottom.

> —Edward M. Kennedy. Speech,
> The National Association of
> Private Industry Councils
> Conference, February 27, 1995.

For decades, the labor movement has stood as a bulwark for freedom and democracy against tyranny around the world. The labor movement was essential in making America a strong society. Its advocacy of progressive legislation has brought immense benefits to all Americans, whether or not they have a union card.

> —*Edward M. Kennedy.*
> *Statement on the North*
> *American Free Trade*
> *Agreement, November 20,*
> *1993.*

Religion

I am an angel. I arise at six o'clock (fifteen minutes earlier than the others) and go to meditation nearly every morning. So you see my piety is increasing.

> —*Rose Fitzgerald. Letter to her*
> *parents from a convent school*
> *in Holland, 1908.*

I'm sure my knees ached and that sometimes I wondered why I should be doing all the kneeling and studying and memorizing and contemplating and praying. But I became understanding and grateful. And in my own time I tried to pass on to my own children this precious gift of faith.

> —*Rose F. Kennedy.* Times to
> Remember, *1974.*

Their mother [Rose] insisted that the girls go to Catholic schools. I had other ideas for the boys' schooling. There is nothing wrong with Catholic schools. They're fine. But I figured the boys could get all the religion they needed in church, and that it would be broadening for them to attend Protestant schools.

> —*Joseph P. Kennedy. Interview,*
> New York Journal-American,
> *July 20, 1960.*

I don't want any of this, John. You must understand. Please don't try. I don't want the thing the priest says not to do.

> —*Kathleen Kennedy. Remark to*
> *suitor John White, 1941.*

I hope that no American . . . will waste his franchise and throw away his vote by voting either for me or against me solely on account of my religious affiliation. It is not relevant.

> —*John F. Kennedy. Quoted in*
> Time, *July 25, 1960.*

Nobody asked me if I was a Catholic when I joined the United States Navy. Nobody asked my brother if he was a Catholic before he climbed into an American bomber plane to fly his last mission.

> —*John F. Kennedy. Campaign*
> *speech, 1960.*

I do not accept the right . . . of any ecclesiastical official to tell me what I shall do in the sphere of my public responsibility as an elected official.

> —*John F. Kennedy. Response to*
> *a question, Houston, Texas,*
> *September 12, 1960.*

I believe in an America where religious intolerance will some-day end—where all men and all churches are treated as equal—where every man has the same right to attend or not attend the church of his choice—where there is no anti-Catholic vote, no bloc voting of any kind—and where Catholics, Protestants, and Jews at both lay and pastoral levels will refrain from those attitudes of disdain and division which so often have marred their works in the past, and promote instead the American ideal of brotherhood.

I am wholly opposed to the state being used by any religious group, Catholic or Protestant, to compel, prohibit, or persecute the free exercise of any other religion. And I hope that you and I condemn with equal fervor those nations which deny their presidency to Protestants and those who deny it to Catholics. And rather than cite the misdeeds of those who differ, I would cite the record of the Catholic church in such nations as Ireland and France—and the independence of such statesmen as Adenauer and de Gaulle.

> —*John F. Kennedy. Campaign speech, Greater Houston Ministerial Association, Houston, Texas, September 12, 1960.*

I think it's so unjust of people to be against Jack because he's a Catholic. He's such a poor Catholic. Now, if it was Bobby, I could understand it.

> —*Jacqueline Kennedy. Comment made during her husband's presidential campaign, 1960.*

We can pray a good deal more at home. We can attend our churches with a good deal more fidelity

> —*John F. Kennedy. Response to the Supreme Court's ban on prayer in public schools, June 1963.*

You can't keep God out of the classroom. God is everywhere.

> —*Ethel Skakel Kennedy to Chief Justice Warren on a plane. The Supreme Court was preparing to decide the issue of school prayer.*

Ultimately, America's answer to the intolerant man is diversity, the very diversity which our heritage of religious freedom has inspired.

> —*Robert F. Kennedy.* The
> Pursuit of Justice, *1964.*

As ambassador to England, Joseph Kennedy spoke at ceremonies honoring Samuel Seabury, the first Episcopal bishop of the United States, in Aberdeen, Scotland, in 1938, while the intentions of Hitler were becoming clear to the world. Although he opposed U.S. involvement in the forthcoming war, he saw clearly the threat Hitler presented.

In certain parts of the world, the profession and practice of religion is being called a political offense. Men and women are being deprived of their natural born citizenship and they are being thrown out of the land of their nativity.

Kennedy contrasted this with the cultures of the United States and Great Britain, which he said were imbued with certain old-fashioned but still useful qualities—respect for the rights of others and for the sanctity of engagements as well as a genuine love of freedom for the individual.

Now we will see how sorry the world is for them.

> —*Joseph P. Kennedy. Quoted in
> the* New York Times,
> *November 22, 1938.*

Kennedy was referring to Jews seeking to leave Nazi Germany in 1938. Kennedy had devised an evacuation plan. However, the plan would have required a massive commitment from the United States and British governments, a fleet of ships, refugee camps, and $150 million to $600 million dollars. The plan was never executed.

Joseph Kennedy was often referred to as an anti-Semite. In a Boston
Globe *interview in May 1944, a reporter asked him directly what he
thought of the charge. Kennedy's response began with the defense that
he had done business with many Jews and had several on his payroll,
of whom he said, "They're good businessmen." He then went on at
length:*

Anti-Semitism is their fight just as anti-Irishism was my
fight and the fight of my fathers in this country; and I'm sorry
to say that many of them actually promote anti-Semitism in
their very efforts to combat it. . . . Whenever I have been asked
for a statement condemning anti-Semitism, I have answered:
"What good would it do?" If the Jews themselves would pay
less attention to advertising their racial problem, and more
attention to solving it, the whole thing would recede into its
proper perspective. It's entirely out of focus now, and that is
chiefly their fault.

*He continued by saying that Jews should be the educators, which will
bring an end to anti-Semitism, and that Jews in public office should
not take criticism as anti-Semitism. He concluded by saying:*

Publicizing unjust attacks upon the Jews may help to cure
the injustice, but continually publicizing the whole problem
only serves to keep it alive in the public mind. A magazine
piece with pictures, extolling the heroism of the Jews in this
war, is all right, until it becomes an unexpected argument
against anti-Semitism, and then a reader of Irish, Swedish, or
Italian descent reacts immediately by saying: "True, but what
about us?" Each race can make out a flattering record in this
war. I happen to be proud of the record of the Irish. Pride in
race is a poor weapon to use in fighting anti-Semitism. I try
to see the whole problem in its proper perspective. If that's
anti-Semitism, then I don't understand the word. That's the
way I feel about it. At least, they can never call me a hypocrite.

*Asked about John F. Kennedy's narrow victory over Richard M. Nixon,
Joseph Kennedy replied:*

I didn't think it would be that close. I was wrong on two things. First, I thought he would get a bigger Catholic vote than he did. Second, I did not think so many would vote against him because of his religion.

> —*Joseph P. Kennedy. Quoted in*
> Life, *December 19, 1960.*

When Mr. Khrushchev reported that the cosmonauts—like the Bolshevik pilots of the early twenties—reported seeing "no signs of God," we can only suggest that they aim—with the rest of mankind—a little higher.

> —*Robert F. Kennedy. Address to*
> *the Center for Study of*
> *Democratic Institutions of the*
> *Fund for the Republic, New*
> *York, January 22, 1963.*

The weakness of man should not weaken the image of God.

> —*John F. Kennedy. Remark, 1962.*

We had a friendly audience with Pope John. He is an impressive man with wonderful humility and a fine sense of humor. He blessed us all, including the American newspapermen who were traveling with us, most of whom were not Catholics. He assured them that it was just a little blessing and wouldn't do them any harm.

> —*Robert F. Kennedy. Comments*
> *on his return from a visit to*
> *Rome, 1962.*

I met this afternoon with members of the American Society of Newspaper Editors in Washington and we got along well, perhaps because some of them realized I used to be a newspaperman myself. I don't think I can lay claim to quite as close a bond at this gathering. Nonetheless, I am pleased and honored to join with you.

> —*Robert F. Kennedy. Speech,*
> *American Jewish Committee*
> *Appeal for Human Relations,*
> *New York City, April 16, 1964.*

The church is . . . at its best only at the time of death. The rest of the time it's often rather silly little men running around in their black suits. But the Catholic church understands death. I'll tell you who else understands death are the black churches. I remember at the funeral of Martin Luther King, I was looking at those faces, and I realized that they knew death. They see it all the time and they're ready for it . . . in the way in which a good Catholic is. We know death. . . . As a matter of fact, if it weren't for the children, we'd welcome it.

> —*Jacqueline Kennedy. Remark after the shooting of Robert F. Kennedy, 1968.*

I guess God has taken care of the problem in His own way, hasn't He?

> —*Kathleen Kennedy. Letter, 1944, on the death of her husband, William Cavendish. Her marriage to a Protestant had caused a family rift.*

The Arts

The happy relationship between the arts and politics which has characterized our long history I think has reached culmination tonight.

> —*John F. Kennedy. Speech at the inaugural ball at the National Gallery of Art, which had featured a stream of writers and performers paying tribute to the new president, January 20, 1960.*

The men who create power make an indispensable contribution to the nation's greatness, but the men who question power make a contribution just as indispensable, especially when that questioning is disinterested, for they determine whether we use power or power uses us.

It is hardly an accident that Robert Frost coupled poetry and power, for he saw poetry as the means of saving power from itself. When power leads man towards arrogance, poetry reminds him of his limitations. When power narrows the areas of man's concern, poetry reminds him of the richness and diversity of his existence. When power corrupts, poetry cleanses.

The artist, however faithful to his personal vision of reality, becomes the last champion of the individual mind and sensibility against an intrusive society and an officious state. The great artist is thus a solitary figure. He has, as Frost said, a lover's quarrel with the world.

In a free society art is not a weapon and it does not belong to the sphere of polemics and ideology. Artists are not engineers of the soul. . . . In serving his vision of the truth, the artist best serves his nation.

—*John F. Kennedy. From a speech at the dedication of the Robert Frost Library. Amherst College, October 26, 1963.*

Everything in the White House must have a reason for being there. It would be a sacrilege merely to redecorate—a word I hate. It must be restored.

—*Jacqueline Kennedy. Remark on her extensive "restoration" of the White House interior.*

You must continue. Poets are the ones who change the world.

—*Jacqueline Kennedy Onassis. Letter to a young poet.*

Our culture and art do not speak to America alone. To the extent that artists struggle to express beauty in form and color and sound, to the extent that they write about man's struggle with nature or society or himself, to that extent they strike a responsive chord in all humanity. . . . Thus today, as always, art knows no national boundaries.

As a democratic society, we have a special responsibility to the arts. For art is the great democrat, calling forth creative genius from every sector of society, disregarding race or religion or wealth or color. The mere accumulation of wealth and power is available to the dictator and the democrat alike. What freedom alone can bring is the liberation of the human mind and spirit, which finds its greatest flowering in the free society.

> —*John F. Kennedy. Speech,*
> *National Cultural Center*
> *dinner, Washington, D.C.,*
> *November 29, 1962.*

Leonardo da Vinci was not only an artist and a sculptor, an architect and a scientist, he was also a military engineer, an occupation which he pursued, he tells us, in order to preserve the chief gift of nature, which is liberty.

> —*John F. Kennedy. Opening of*
> Mona Lisa *exhibition,*
> *National Gallery of Art,*
> *Washington, D.C., January 8,*
> *1963.*

Poverty and Public Assistance

You're lucky. You've been poor.

> —*Robert F. Kennedy. Remark to*
> *a friend.*

The state means to most untrained minds some vast, nebulous institution which will somehow or other assume all the burdens of life and support the individual who lacks the ambition or energy to support himself

> —*Joseph P. Kennedy. Speech to Boy Scout leaders, Long Island, New York, October 1945.*

Seventeen million Americans, who live over sixty-five on an average Social Security check of about seventy-eight dollars a month, they're not able to sustain themselves individually, but they can sustain themselves through the Social Security system. I don't believe in big government, but I believe in effective governmental action.

> —*John F. Kennedy. Opening statement, first Kennedy-Nixon debate, Chicago, September 26, 1960.*

To those people in the huts and villages of half the globe struggling to break the bonds of mass misery, we pledge our best efforts to help them help themselves, for whatever period is required, not because the Communists may be doing it, not because we seek their votes, but because it is right. If a free society cannot help the many who are poor, it cannot save the few who are rich.

> —*John F. Kennedy. Inaugural address, January 20, 1961.*

Any veteran who watched the American supplies pouring onshore at the Normandy beaches; who saw Pacific islands cleared and airstrips rolled in four or five days; who saw the endless waste of war and the seemingly never-ending productivity that replaced the waste. . . . Is it any wonder that the veteran cannot understand why he is not housed?

> —*John F. Kennedy. Address to Congress as a representative in support of the Wagner-Elender-Taft Bill, designed to construct fifteen million low-income houses.*

I believe that, as long as there is plenty, poverty is evil. Government belongs wherever evil needs an adversary and there are people in distress who cannot help themselves.

> —*Robert F. Kennedy. Speech, 1964.*

In many ways Wall Street is closer to London than it is to Harlem, a few miles uptown. Scarsdale is often closer to Paris than Selma, Alabama; and Americans in Appalachia are in many ways closer to the Favelas of Rio de Janeiro than they are to the society in which you and I live.

> —*Robert F. Kennedy. Speech, testimonial dinner for Congressman John Down, Sterling Forest, New York, May 2, 1965.*

The war on poverty, like or not, is the single outstanding commitment this nation has made to the principle that poverty must be abolished. Not just that fathers shall not be without jobs; and children without education; and mothers without medical care—though it is all of these. The war on poverty is a commitment to the principle that every American shall have the same opportunities to make a life for himself and for his own children—and the same opportunity to share in the government of his city and state and country, the same opportunity to share in the great enterprises of American public life.

> —*Robert F. Kennedy. Senate speech, October 3, 1966.*

Welfare workers, or higher welfare payments, cannot confer self-respect or self-confidence in men without work—for in the United States, you are what you do.

> —*Robert F. Kennedy. Address, Borough Presidents' Conference of Community Leaders, January 21, 1966.*

Of all the programs and services that have stripped the poor of their dignity and treated them as a nation apart, public assistance is foremost. It is . . . wholly inadequate, both in what it provides and the number of people it helps.

> —*Robert F. Kennedy.* To Seek a Newer World, *1967.*

The great unmentioned problem of America today is the growth, rapid and insidious, of a group in our midst, perhaps more dangerous, more bereft of hope, more difficult to confront, than any for which our history has prepared us. It is a group that threatens to become what America has never known—a permanent underclass.

> —*Edward M. Kennedy. Speech, May 7, 1978.*

Our public housing efforts over the years, important and successful as they have been, have never succeeded in erasing the plight of those entrapped in slum housing. I would venture to say that one reason for this—although I do not want to oversimplify—is that the federal government has never had a program for low-income housing which has involved private enterprise in a meaningful way.

> —*Robert F. Kennedy. Remarks to The New York State Home Builders Association, October 15, 1965.*

Reliance on government is dependence—and what the people of our ghettos need is not greater dependence, but full independence; not the charity of and favor of their fellow citizens, but equal claims of right and equal power to enforce those claims.

> —*Robert F. Kennedy. Address, NAACP Legal Defense Fund banquet, New York City, May 18, 1966.*

The crisis in employment is the most critical of our failures. It is both measure and cause of the extent to which the poor man is alienated from the general community. More than segregation in housing and schools, more than differences in attitude or life style, it is unemployment that sets the urban poor apart. Unemployment is having nothing to do—which means having nothing to do with the rest of us.

—*Robert F. Kennedy.* To Seek a Newer World, *1967.*

Society's dissatisfactions with too much government are often translated into dissatisfaction with the people in government.

—*Edward M. Kennedy. Speech, May 11, 1977.*

Liberals must stop viewing government as the caretaker of first resort.

—*Kathleen Kennedy Townsend. Quoted in* U.S. News and World Report *profile, December 16, 1985.*

A federal program is not the solution to every problem. But there continues to be an important federal role in solving the problems of our society by investing in people and the infrastructure needed for our country to succeed and our citizens to thrive. To believe otherwise is hostile to the basic values of our country and to the historic concept of "We the People" in our Constitution. We must not rob the people of the resource of government. It is their government, and we must make it work for them.

—*Edward M. Kennedy. Speech, National Press Club, Washington, D.C., January 11, 1995.*

There has been a steady drumbeat of loud calls for cutting welfare benefits by some in this Congress. But there has been a deafening silence on the need for child care. It is time to break the silence and put together a realistic reform—reform based not on rhetoric, but on results.

> —*Edward M. Kennedy.*
> *Statement, March 1, 1995.*

When we find that 65 percent of the public school students in Boston are growing up in poverty while we are spending billions on defense, something is wrong. Believe me, ladies and gentlemen, that something is not wrong with America. It's wrong with our leaders.

> —*Joseph P. Kennedy II. Victory*
> *speech celebrating his election*
> *to Congress, September 16,*
> *1986.*

Health Care

Medicare fulfilled a dream of a generation's standing, for social progress moves slowly and statutory reforms often lag behind scientific achievement and popular will. . . . But Medicare also imposes a great responsibility on us. It summons us to the task of ensuring not only that the cost of medical care is no longer a burden upon those who need but cannot afford it, but that good medical care itself is available. The bright hopes of Medicare can be dashed if we fail to achieve this availability. . . . Unless we as a nation are prepared, right now, to ensure that we have the facilities needed to implement the Medicare legislation, we would almost have been better off to have done nothing.

> —*Robert F. Kennedy. Address,*
> *American Medical Center, Judy*
> *Holliday Memorial Dinner,*
> *New York City, May 15,*
> *1966.*

If we deny the finest health care to any citizens, we deny the value of their lives. They become slaves of unnecessary suffering and disability. The promise of a bountiful society acquires a hollow ring. The American dream becomes a nightmare.

—*Edward M. Kennedy. Speech,*
October 5, 1975.

America doesn't need a double standard of health care—one for those who can afford it and another for those who can't.

—*Edward M. Kennedy. Speech,*
February 1, 1976.

With the sole exception of South Africa, no other industrialized nation in the world leaves its citizens in fear of financial ruin because of illness.

—*Edward M. Kennedy. Senate*
speech, December 9, 1978.

What we have today in the United States is not so much a health-care system as a disease-cure system.

—*Edward M. Kennedy. Speech,*
May 31, 1979.

Thirty-one years ago this summer, Dr. Martin Luther King led the March on Washington to demand basic human rights for all Americans. Today we have the chance to fulfill another part of that dream, by making health care a basic right.

—*Edward M. Kennedy.*
Statement on Health Care
Reform, July 28, 1994.

Medicare and Social Security are two of the most successful programs ever enacted. They are a solemn commitment to all Americans—North, South, East, and West—that if they contribute to the trust funds during their working years, they will

have financial security and health security in their golden
years.

—*Edward M. Kennedy. Speech,*
Medicare Thirtieth
Anniversary Celebration, July
25, 1995.

The Republicans' attack on Medicare will make life harder,
sicker, and shorter for millions of elderly Americans who built
this country and made it great. They deserve better.

—*Edward M. Kennedy.*
Statement on the Amendment
to Restore Medicare Funding,
October 25, 1995.

As the crisis continues, it becomes more and more difficult
for anyone to pretend that AIDS is someone else's problem.
There are few of us who do not know someone who is either
infected or affected by AIDS. In a very real way, we are all
living with AIDS.

—*Edward M. Kennedy.*
Statement, May 14, 1996.

Drugs, Tobacco, and Alcohol

I believe we must take a significantly greater action to dis-
courage people from smoking at all and especially to discour-
age young people from starting to smoke.

—*Robert F. Kennedy. Statement*
on Health Hazards of
Cigarette Smoking, May 17,
1967.

One physician told me recently that if he had his choice as
a matter of health policy between immediately having enough
doctors and nurses and hospital beds to remedy our serious
national shortages in these areas, and getting every American
who smokes cigarettes to stop, he would choose the latter. Far

more lives, he told me, would be saved by getting the forty-eight million Americans who now smoke to stop than would be saved by solving all of our health, power, and facility shortages.

> —Robert F. Kennedy. Statement
> on Health Hazards of
> Cigarette Smoking, May 17,
> 1967.

Some 75 percent of those addicted to heroin come from the 20 percent of society with the lowest incomes. Until there are enough jobs to go around, until everyone has a decent home and a decent education, until we have uniformly stable and secure family structures—in short, until the world is a much better place than it is now—the mental problems associated with addiction—and addiction itself in one form or another—will continue to occur.

> —Robert F. Kennedy. Speech,
> Union Baptist Church, New
> York City, December 6, 1965.

It is hard to convince an addict that there really is hope, that he should seriously commit himself to a program which seeks to make him a member of a society that never before did anything good for him.

> —Robert F. Kennedy. Senate
> speech, June 9, 1965.

The turn to drugs is really just a symptom of something much deeper and broader in our nation—an alienation which threatens the security of young people and parents and society as a whole. . . .

Short kicks are increasingly attractive when the long-run picture is bleak—when we may not be here at all, or when the same old hypocrisies prevail if we are.

> —Edward M. Kennedy. Address,
> Massachusetts Teachers
> Association, Boston, May 2,
> 1970.

For those who are users but not pushers—for our many young people today who have grown up in a drug culture and are experimenting with drugs—the emphasis should be on prevention and rehabilitation, not simply throwing them in jail. We should not automatically burden these youngsters with the albatross of a criminal felony conviction to wear for the rest of their lives.

> —*Edward M. Kennedy.*
> *Statement, October 7, 1970.*

As a teenager, I started down the wrong path in dealing with the pressures of growing up. I mistakenly believed that experimenting with drugs and alcohol could alleviate them. I finally decided not to escape from those pressures, but to confront them.

> —*Patrick J. Kennedy. Son of*
> *Edward Kennedy, and then a*
> *state representative for Rhode*
> *Island. Public statement,*
> *quoted in the* Boston Globe,
> *December 10, 1991.*

It is about time that the administration realize what the American people have known for some time: that the alcohol industry is not about to change its tune voluntarily.

> —*Joseph P. Kennedy II. Quoted*
> *in* Alcoholism & Drug Abuse
> Week, *November 6, 1991.*

People who do not think there is a problem with young people drinking alcohol in this country do not understand the facts. Let us put an end to trying to market children a drug that unnecessarily kills far too many of our nation's most vital resources.

> —*Joseph P. Kennedy II.*
> *Statement introducing a bill to*
> *curb alcohol advertising.*
> *Quoted in* Alcoholism & Drug
> Abuse Week, *May 20, 1996.*

We spend billions and billions to fight drugs but, comparatively, spend nothing against alcohol. And alcohol is a drug.

> —*Joseph P. Kennedy II.*
> *Comments on why there*
> *should be warnings in all*
> *alcohol ads. Quoted in*
> Advertising Age, *July 16,*
> *1990.*

There's a price to pay, whether it's a hangover the next morning or alcoholism five years later or a drug habit five years later. There's always a price to pay.

> —*Christopher Lawford, first*
> *child of Patricia Kennedy and*
> *Peter Lawford, founder of*
> *North Charles Mental Health*
> *Clinic, and lecturer in*
> *psychiatry, Harvard Medical*
> *School.*

·4·

Government

Democracy

Democracy is the superior form of government, because it is based on a respect for a man as a reasonable being.

—*John F. Kennedy.* Why
England Slept, *1940.*

Democracy is a difficult kind of government. It requires the highest qualities of self-discipline, restraint, a willingness to make commitments and sacrifices for the general interest, and it also requires knowledge.

—*John F. Kennedy. Speech,
Dublin Castle, Ireland,
June 28, 1963.*

Before my term has ended we shall have to test whether a nation organized as our own can endure. . . . Each day the crises multiply. Each day the solution becomes more difficult. Each day we draw nearer to the hour of maximum danger.

—*John F. Kennedy. State of the
Union Address, January 30,
1961.*

Democracy cannot be imposed by force or otherwise. It would not last even if we were able to present [other nations] with the most up-to-date constitutional system. In our very attempt at this colossal crusade we would end in failure and disgrace abroad, in disillusionment and bankruptcy at home.

—*Joseph P. Kennedy. Speech,
Oglethorpe University,
Atlanta, May 1941.*

Democracy is never a final achievement. It is by nature an ever-changing challenge, a call to untiring effort, to renewed dedication, to new goals to meet the needs of each new generation.

—*Robert F. Kennedy. Speech.*

Many voices, many views, all have combined into an American consensus, and it has been a consensus of good sense. "In the multitude of counselors, there is safety," says the Bible, and so it is with American democracy. Tolerance is an expression of trust in that consensus, and each new enlargement of tolerance is an enlargement of democracy.

—*Robert F. Kennedy. Speech,
dedication of the John F.
Kennedy Interfaith Chapel,
West Georgia College,
Carrollton, Georgia,
May 26, 1964.*

[We are] not a continent, not an arsenal, not wealth and factories—but a democratic republic. Call it democracy or freedom; call it human liberty or individual opportunity, equality or justice. But underneath they are all the same—the belief in the right and capacity of every individual to govern himself, and to share in governing the necessary institutions of social order.

—*Edward M. Kennedy. Speech,
May 14, 1978.*

Power

You want power because it's an opportunity.

—*Edward M. Kennedy.
Remark, 1980.*

Wealth is the means and people are the ends.

> —*John F. Kennedy. Attributed.*

John F. Kennedy was once asked why he wanted to be president. His reply was straightforward:

Because that's where the power is.

> —*John F. Kennedy. Quoted in* Time, *November 29, 1963.*

I think I had my maximum impact the way I had it. I couldn't have done more as a man, or in some position. You know I don't know what else I could have done. I was perfectly happy where I was. And I think I just had a very wonderful relationship with my brother, and he was wonderful to this cause. I don't say that blindly.

> —*Eunice Kennedy Shriver. Comments on her mostly behind-the-scenes role in the Kennedy White House, where she was consultant to the President's Panel on Mental Retardation. Quoted in Laurence Leamer,* The Kennedy Women, *1994.*

In the context of the civil rights movement, Robert Kennedy was asked if the federal government should have stepped in more frequently as law enforcer. Kennedy replied:

I just wouldn't want that much more authority in the hands of either the FBI or the Department of Justice or the president of the United States. . . . We could have sent perhaps large numbers of people down to Mississippi and be able then to protect that group down there. But I think that it comes back to haunt you at a later time. I think that these matters should be decided over a long range of history, not on a temporary basis or under the stress of a particular crisis. . . . I think it's best for the health of the country.

> —Robert F. Kennedy. Interview
> for JFK Oral History,
> December 1964.

I have influence because I have contacts with Averell Harriman and I'm on the counterintelligence committee . . . but the influence is just infinitesimal compared to the influence I had before [John F. Kennedy was killed].

> —Robert F. Kennedy.
> Interview, 1964.

I'm not just a senator. I'm senator from New York. I'm head of the Kennedy wing of the party.

> —Robert F. Kennedy. Robert F.
> Kennedy Oral History.

It seems to me that the idea of a family serving in the government generation after generation, as is the case with so many English families as well, is one we might do well to think about and encourage in our own country.

> —Rose F. Kennedy. Journal
> entry, May 21, 1941.

Won't it be wonderful when we get back in the White House?

> —Jacqueline Kennedy. Remark
> to Ethel and Robert Kennedy
> during the 1968 presidential
> primaries.

The consumer is the only man in our economy without a high-powered lobbyist in Washington.

> —*John F. Kennedy. Campaign speech, Wittenberg College, Springfield, Ohio, 1960.*

The essential humanity of men can be protected and preserved only where government must answer—not just to the wealthy; not just to those of a particular religion, or a particular race; but to all its people. And even government by the consent of the governed, as in our own Constitution, must be limited in its power to act against its people.

> —*Robert F. Kennedy. Address, Day of Affirmation, University of Capetown, June 6, 1966.*

A nation as rich and powerful as my own, and so fortunate in its history, is tempted to believe that all problems, no matter how complex, can be solved by pulling on the levers of power or pushing the buttons of solution.

> —*Edward M. Kennedy. Speech, Trinity College Historical Society Bicentennial, Dublin, Ireland, March 3, 1970.*

[The shooting at Kent State] has stripped away the fragile cover of hypocrisy and reassurance from the turbulent unrest of American life. It has illuminated the corruption of obsolete dogmas. It tells us that power which is arrogant or indifferent is at war with the liberation of the human spirit; that power unrestrained by moral values of the people—as they themselves see those needs—must either perish or maintain itself by force.

> —*Edward M. Kennedy. Statement on the Kent State shootings, May 8, 1970.*

Rarely, if ever, in our history have private-interest groups been better organized, better financed, or more resistant to the force of change. It was Lord Bryce who commented in the nineteenth century that American government was all engine and no brakes. Today it could be said . . . that our government is all brakes and no engine.

> —Edward M. Kennedy,
> September 22, 1978.

Politics and Politicians

I never would have imagined before the war that I would become active in politics.

> —John F. Kennedy, 1960.

Mothers may want their sons to grow up the become president, but they don't want them to become politicians in the process.

> —John F. Kennedy. Attributed.

I don't want my brother to get mixed up with politicians!

> —Robert F. Kennedy. Remark to
> Democrats in a "back room"
> meeting during John F.
> Kennedy's Senate campaign,
> 1952.

I must be nuts. The two men in public life I love most are Jack and you. And I disagree with you guys more than anyone else. What's wrong with me?

> —Joseph P. Kennedy. Remark to
> William O. Douglas. Quoted in
> his book, Go East, Young
> Man, 1974.

Joseph P. Kennedy Jr. was a delegate at the Democratic National Convention of 1940, with a delegation pledged to James A. Farley. At the convention, great pressure was placed to get him to switch to Roosevelt. He resisted, and his father cabled Farley, thanking him for his cable.

As you can imagine I had heard about the struggle to get him to change his vote and was delighted he took the stand he did. After all, if he is going into politics he might just as well learn now that the only thing to do is to stand by your convictions. Am most happy to say he needed no prompting in this respect.

> —*Joseph P. Kennedy. Quoted in Rose F. Kennedy,* Times to Remember, *1974.*

Washington is a city of Southern efficiency and Northern charm.

> —*John F. Kennedy. Remark. Quoted in William Manchester,* Portrait of a President, *1962.*

The desire to be reelected exercises a strong brake on independent courage.

> —*John F. Kennedy.*

We came into this administration without a political obligation. . . . I don't mean that people didn't do favors for us and that we wanted to do favors for them. [But] there weren't any promises made to anyone that they would get a job. . . . There were certainly no cabinet positions promised. . . . It was really a fresh slate.

> —*Robert F. Kennedy. Interview, February 29, 1964.*

John F. Kennedy on how his views had changed from the time he was a representative:

I'd just come out of my father's house at the time, and these were the things I knew.

—*Quoted in William
Manchester,* Portrait of a
President, *1962.*

When asked why he chose politics over business, John F. Kennedy replied:

The political world is so much more stimulating. It's the most interesting thing you can do—it beats following the dollar. It's a very interesting life. It allows the full use of your powers. First there is the great chess game. It's the battle, the competition. There's the strategy and which piece you move and all that. And then in government you can do something about what you think.

—*John F. Kennedy. Interview,*
Time, *November 7, 1960.*

After being soundly defeated in an attempt to win the vice-presidential nomination at the 1956 Democratic National Convention, John F. Kennedy called his father:

We did our best. I had fun and I didn't make a fool of myself.

—*John F. Kennedy. Quoted in*
Life, *December 19, 1960.*

Robert's take on the 1956 convention:

You're better off than you ever were in your life, and you made a great fight, and they're not going to win and you're going to be the candidate the next time.

—*Robert F. Kennedy. Remark to
John F. Kennedy.*

In the last year I got to know a lot of famous people—senators and so on—very well, and I found that they are not always what they should be.

—*Jean Kennedy Smith. Quoted in* Time, *June 7, 1960.*

Politicians do nothing but hold meetings. . . . You can't get any work out of a politician.

—*Robert F. Kennedy. Interview on John F. Kennedy's 1952 campaign.*

I am getting out of all political activities as fast as I can. Partisan politics played no role when I was chief counsel for the McClellan Labor-Rackets Committee. They will play no part now.

—*Robert F. Kennedy. Interview after taking over as attorney general,* Look, *March 22, 1961.*

You can't tell the public to go to hell anymore. Fifty men have run America, and that's a high figure. The rest of America is demanding a share in the game, and they'll get it.

—*Joseph P. Kennedy. Interview, the* New York Times, *July 26, 1936.*

I thought that I had become such a liability and the campaign [against the Kennedys] was getting so bitter and mean. . . . People were saying so many things and it was getting more and more of the family.

—*Robert F. Kennedy, on his mood in the fall of 1963. Robert F. Kennedy Oral History, JFK Memorial Library.*

If I ran for president . . . I would not strengthen the . . . dialogue that is taking place in connection with these issues [Vietnam], but in fact I would weaken it. It would immediately become a personality struggle between me, as an overly ambitious figure trying to take the nomination away from President Johnson, who deserves it because of the fact that he is not only president but served the Democratic party and the country as president for four or five years.

> —Robert F. Kennedy.
> Appearance on Face the
> Nation, November 26, 1967.

From here on, you must think of Jack less as a friend and more as a potential candidate for the presidency of the United States.

> —Joseph P. Kennedy. Remark to
> Lem Billings, a lifelong friend
> of the Kennedys, 1957.

No more speeches for me. Jack's going into politics.

> —Joseph P. Kennedy. Response
> to a request for a
> speech, 1945.

There are no accidents in politics.

> —Joseph P. Kennedy. Remark to
> a reporter, 1960.

There are only two pursuits that get in your blood—politics and the motion-picture business.

> —Joseph P. Kennedy. Remark to
> a friend. Quoted in Time,
> August 12, 1940.

I have no presidential aspirations. Nor does my wife, Ethel Bird.

> —*Robert F. Kennedy. Remark,*
> *fall 1967.*

I don't want them to inherit my enemies. It's tough enough they inherit my friends.

> —*Joseph P. Kennedy to Morton*
> *Downey, on why he was*
> *deliberately fading from public*
> *view in the late 1950s.*

You judge a person by the friends they keep. You also judge a person by the enemies they make. On that score, I think I have made the right enemies.

> —*Patrick J. Kennedy. On his*
> *years as a Rhode Island state*
> *representative. Quoted in the*
> Christian Science Monitor,
> *August 29, 1994.*

Frequently events matter less than . . . spin control—who in which campaign can explain why something doesn't mean what it seems.

> —*Edward M. Kennedy.*

To a person in public life, nothing is more distressing today than the massive cynicism, hostility, and outright distrust that is undermining the people's basic faith and confidence in government and its institutions.

> —*Edward M. Kennedy. Speech,*
> *September 10, 1976.*

I don't think you're going to be a success in anything if you think about losing, whether it's in sports or in politics.

> —*Edward M. Kennedy. Quoted*
> *in Lee Green,* Sportswit,
> *1984.*

If your enemies see this picture of us together, I'm in big trouble.

> —*Edward M. Kennedy to*
> *Senator James G. Abourezk*
> *during a photo shoot.*

My uncle Jack and my father always used to quote that Englishman—politics is the noblest profession. To me, politics is crap. That's the main thing, maybe the only thing I've learned in my life. American needs a rest from the Kennedys and vice versa.

> —*David A. Kennedy. In an*
> *interview.*

But all his life, my father felt deeply about politics, that in fact it was an honorable profession. I think probably his proudest legacy is that, during the time he was president and in the years after he died, people who normally wouldn't have chosen a political career or involved themselves in politics suddenly had a new feeling about politics and public service. Therefore, they got involved and committed themselves.

> —*John F. Kennedy Jr. Speech*
> *announcing the Profiles in*
> *Courage awards, 1990.*

Politics is, after all, a service industry.

> —*John F. Kennedy Jr. Editor's*
> *letter,* George,
> *September 1996.*

ROBERT F. KENNEDY, "RUTHLESS POLITICIAN"

People say I am ruthless. I am *not* ruthless. And if I find the man who is calling me ruthless, I shall destroy him.

> —*Robert F. Kennedy, during his Senate campaign, New York City, 1964.*

All this for a ruthless man? Just think of what they'd do for a kind one.

> —*Robert F. Kennedy, on the mobs of supporters that appeared at his campaign stops during the presidential primaries, 1968.*

If I was really ruthless, I'd find a way to get even with the *Times*.

> —*Robert F. Kennedy, after the* New York Times *called his victory in Indiana during the primaries "inconclusive," 1968.*

That's my good deed for the day. Now I can go back to being ruthless.

> —*Robert F. Kennedy. Remark to a friend after he brought the newspaper inside to his wife.*

Now I can go back to being ruthless again.

> —*Robert F. Kennedy, after winning his Senate campaign, November 1964.*

Upon hearing that a well-known Washingtonian had called him a "vicious little monster":

Tell him I'm not so little!

HENRY CABOT LODGE

When you've beaten him, you've beaten the best. Why try for something else?

> —*Joseph P. Kennedy. Remark on Senator Henry Cabot Lodge, whom John Kennedy would unseat in the 1952 Senate race.*

At last, the Fitzgeralds have evened the score with the Lodges.

> —*Rose Kennedy. Remark after the 1952 Senate race. Henry Lodge's grandfather had beat Rose's grandfather in a Senate race thirty-six years earlier by thirty thousand votes.*

THE NIXONS

We know that it will not be easy to campaign against a man who has spoken or voted on every known side of every known issue. Mr. Nixon may feel it is his turn now, after the New Deal and the Fair Deal—but before he deals, someone had better cut the cards.

> —*John F. Kennedy. Acceptance speech, Democratic National Convention, Los Angeles, California, July 15, 1960.*

I'm sure I spend less than Mrs. Nixon on clothes. She gets hers at Elizabeth Arden, and nothing there costs less than $200 or $300.

> —*Jacqueline Kennedy. Interview, Associated Press, September 15, 1960.*

FRANKLIN DELANO ROOSEVELT

I'll take any job you want me to and even work for nothing so long as it's interesting. I never want to be bored.

—*Joseph P. Kennedy. Letter to Franklin Delano Roosevelt, 1936.*

I can say no to that fellow on the telephone, but face-to-face he gets me

—*Joseph P. Kennedy. Remark on Franklin Delano Roosevelt, 1936.*

I must confess that I was as susceptible as most people to Roosevelt's charm and blandishments. He was undoubtedly a genius in his personal relationships. He knew that one of the easiest ways to get around me was to tell me complimentary things about my father. I knew what he was doing. . . . Nevertheless, even while I knew I was being charmed, the charm was difficult to resist.

—*Rose F. Kennedy.* Times to Remember, *1974.*

Roosevelt was a man of action. He had the capacity to get things done. . . . Long before the campaign, long before his name was even seriously considered, I went out to work for him. I think I was the first man with more than $12 in the bank who openly supported him. I did this because I had seen him in action. I knew what he could do and how he did it, and I felt that after a long period of inactivity we needed a leader who would lead.

—*Joseph P. Kennedy. Quoted in the* New York Times, *August 12, 1934.*

I knew that big drastic changes had to be made in our economic system, and I felt that Roosevelt was the one who could make these changes. I wanted him in the White House for my own security and for the security of our kids, and I was ready to do anything to help elect him.

> —*Joseph P. Kennedy. Quoted in Joe McCarthy*, The Remarkable Kennedys, *1960.*

On Roosevelt's as-then-unannounced third term:

I can't go against the guy. He's done more for me than my own kind. If he wants it, I'll be with him.

> —*Joseph Kennedy. Off-record remark to a friendly reporter, 1939.*

Just two days later, Kennedy, speaking from the steps of the White House, made his support for Roosevelt's third term official:

The problems that are going to affect the people of the United States—political, social, and economic—are already so great and becoming greater by the war that they should be handled by a man it won't take two years to educate.

First and foremost, we know from what we have seen and heard that President Roosevelt's policy is to keep us out of war, and war at this time would bring to this country chaos beyond anybody's dreams. This, in my opinion, overshadows any possible objection to a third term.

> —*Quoted in the* New York Times, *December 9, 1939.*

It is true that there have been disagreements between the president and me—I have disagreed with him on methods employed in carrying out objectives on which we were agreed. . . . However, there are times, as you all know, which clamor for national unity—times when national teamwork is vital and when only fundamental disagreements should be considered.

—*Joseph P. Kennedy. Radio*
address endorsing Roosevelt,
October 29, 1940.

A greater love hath no man than he who gives his life for his country. As a member of President Roosevelt's official family for many years, I know that he felt that justice had been violated seriously by this war, and he had dedicated his life that the grave injuries to states and inhabitants should be rectified.

—*Joseph P. Kennedy. Tribute to*
Roosevelt, Washington
Evening-Star, *April 13, 1945.*

Soon after taking over the presidency, John F. Kennedy was asked about comparisons made between himself and Roosevelt. His answer was terse:

There is no validity to the comparison.

—*John F. Kennedy. Quoted in*
William Manchester, Portrait
of a President, *1962.*

SENATOR JOE McCARTHY

In case there is any question in your mind, I liked Joe McCarthy. I always liked him. . . . He was always pleasant, never a crab. If somebody was against him, he never tried to cut his heart out. He never said anyone was a stinker. He was a pleasant fellow.

I thought he would be a sensation. He was smart. But he went off the deep end.

—*Joseph P. Kennedy. Interview,*
New York Post, *January 9,*
1961.

Robert F. Kennedy worked for Senator Joseph McCarthy for six months in 1952–1953. He was not in the end pleased with the way investigations were conducted.

I told him I thought he was out of his mind and was going to destroy himself. . . . He destroyed himself for that—for publicity. He had to get his name in the paper. . . . He was on a toboggan. It was so exciting and exhilarating as he went downhill that it didn't matter to him if he hit a tree at the bottom.

> —*Robert F. Kennedy. Quoted in R. E. Thompson and Hortense Myers,* Robert F. Kennedy: The Brother Within, *1962.*

When asked by writer Peter Maas how he could have worked for McCarthy, Robert Kennedy replied:

Well, at the time, I thought there was a serious internal security threat to the United States; I felt at that time that Joe McCarthy seemed to be the only one who was doing anything about it. I was wrong.

> —*Robert F. Kennedy. Quoted in Jean Stein and George Plimpton,* American Journey: The Times of Robert Kennedy, *1970.*

Further reflections on McCarthy by Robert:

I liked him and yet time he was terribly heavy-handed. He was a very complicated character. His whole method of operation was complicated because he would get a guilty feeling and get hurt after he had blasted somebody. He wanted so desperately to be liked. . . . He was sensitive and yet insensitive. He didn't anticipate the results of what he was doing. He was very thoughtful of his friends, and yet he could be so cruel to others.

I felt sorry for him, particularly in the last year, when he was such a beaten, destroyed person, particularly since many of his so-called friends, realizing he was finished, ran away from him and left him with virtually no one.

> —*Robert F. Kennedy. Quoted in*
> *R. E. Thompson and Hortense*
> *Myers,* Robert F. Kennedy:
> The Brother Within, *1962.*

Being anti-communist does not automatically excuse a lack of integrity in every other facet of life.

> —*Robert F. Kennedy. Letter to*
> *Robert M. Harriss, January*
> *31, 1955.*

Joe McCarthy, you're a shit.

> —*John F. Kennedy, after*
> *hanging up on Senator*
> *McCarthy over his attempt to*
> *block one of Kennedy's*
> *appointments, 1954.*

When asked, well after McCarthy's death, why he didn't fully partici-pate in the censure of McCarthy, Jack "came clean":

The Joe McCarthy thing? I was caught in a bad situation. My brother [Bobby] was working for Joe. I was against it, I didn't want him to work for Joe, but he wanted to. And how could I get up there and denounce Joe McCarthy when my own brother was working for him? So it wasn't so much a thing of political liability as it was a personal problem.

. . . I had never known the sort of people who were called before the McCarthy committee. I agree that many of them were seriously manhandled, but they all represented a different world to me. What I mean is, I did not identify with them, and so I did not get as worked up as other liberals did.

> —*John F. Kennedy. Interview,*
> *quoted in Ralph G. Martin*
> *and Ed Plaut,* Front Runner,
> Dark Horse, *1960.*

The Presidency

So you want this fucking job.

> —*John F. Kennedy to Senator*
> *Barry M. Goldwater during*
> *the Bay of Pigs affair. Quoted*
> *in Woodward and Bernstein,*
> The Final Days, *1976.*

You know, this job might even be fun if the world weren't in such a mess.

> —*John F. Kennedy.*
> *Remark, 1961.*

Asked in a press conference if he would run for president all over again and if he could recommend the job to others, President Kennedy replied:

Well, the answer . . . to the first is yes and the second is no. I don't recommend it to others—at least for a while.

> —*John F. Kennedy. News*
> *conference, Washington, D.C.,*
> *March 29, 1962.*

If a president breaks his oath, he is not only committing a crime against the Constitution, for which the Congress can impeach and should impeach him, but he is committing a sin against his God.

> —*John F. Kennedy. Television*
> *interview, 1960.*

Asked about his perceptions of the presidency after his first year in office, Kennedy replied:

The responsibilities placed on the United States are greater than I imagined them to be, and there are greater limitations upon our ability to bring about a favorable result than I had imagined them to be. And I think this is probably true of anyone who becomes president, because there is such a difference between those who advise or speak or legislate, and between the man who must select from the various alternatives proposed and say that this shall be the policy of the United States.

The other point is something that President Eisenhower said to me on January nineteenth [1961]. He said, "There are no easy matters that will ever come to you as president. If they are easy, they will be settled at a lower level." So the matters that come to you as president are always the difficult matters, and matters that carry with them large implications.

> —*John F. Kennedy. Television and radio interview, "Year-end Conversation with the President," Washington, D.C., December 17, 1962.*

I don't mind not being president; I just mind that someone else is.

> —*Edward M. Kennedy. Speech, Gridiron Club, Washington, D.C., March 22, 1986.*

If anyone is crazy enough to want to kill a president of the United States, he can do it. All he must be prepared to do is give his life for the president's.

> —*John F. Kennedy. Quoted in Pierre Salinger,* With Kennedy, *1966.*

I'm not going to die in office, so the vice presidency doesn't mean a thing.

> —*John F. Kennedy, defending his decision to take Johnson as a running mate in a private conversation, 1960.*

Congress

They even cut your hair free of charge.

> —*John F. Kennedy. Remark to his family when he first entered the Senate, 1953.*

Man, you could make a lot of friends real fast on those supercommittees.

> —*Joseph P. Kennedy II. Comment on the major congressional committees of the House. Quoted in* Spy, *February 1989.*

I've had a tough time learning how to act like a Congressman. Today, I actually spent some of my own money.

> —*Joseph P. Kennedy II. Quoted in* Newsweek, *February 9, 1987.*

I just never felt like I was accomplishing anything. I was very disappointed, mostly with myself, that I just couldn't get the job done, no matter how hard I tried, no matter how much of myself I would give to the job. I just couldn't get it done.

> —*Joseph P. Kennedy II. Remarks on his early career in Congress. Quoted in the* Boston Globe Magazine, *May 23, 1993.*

It is a pleasure to return from whence I came. You are among my oldest friends in Washington—and this House is my oldest home. . . . To speak from this historic rostrum is a sobering experience. To be back among so many friends is a happy one.

> —*John F. Kennedy. State of the Union Address, January 30, 1961.*

It is much easier in many ways for me . . . when Congress is not in town.

—John F. Kennedy. Press conference, Washington, D.C., June 28, 1962.

But today, were I to offer—after a little more than a week in office—detailed legislation to remedy every national ill, the Congress would rightly wonder whether the desire for speed had replaced the duty of responsibility.

—John F. Kennedy. State of the Union Address, January 30, 1961.

We've got to hit the country while the country's hot. That's the only thing that makes any impression to these goddamned senators. . . . We don't want to wait just for their convenience. . . . They'll move as the country moves.

—John F. Kennedy, discussing the Limited Test Ban Treaty with U.S. Secretary of State Dean Rusk, 1963.

Wilbur Mills knows that he was chairman of Ways and Means before I got here and that he'll still be chairman after I've gone—and he knows I know it.

—John F. Kennedy. Quoted in Theodore Sorenson, Kennedy, 1965.

We're just worms. Nobody pays attention to us nationally.

—John F. Kennedy on his role as a U.S. representative.

Thomas Jefferson once said that he cared not who made a country's laws, so long as he could write its newspapers. If this Congress goes on much longer, I'd rather be in the newspaper business, too.

> —*Robert F. Kennedy. Speech,*
> *New York, October 9, 1965.*

Representative government on Capitol Hill is in the worst shape I have seen it in my sixteen years in the Senate. The heart of the problem is that the Senate and the House of Representatives are awash in a sea of special-interest campaign contributions and special-interest lobbying.

> —*Edward M. Kennedy. Speech,*
> *October 23, 1978.*

Members of Congress cannot live by political-action committees alone.

> —*Edward M. Kennedy. Speech,*
> *April 30, 1979.*

Part of the larger challenge we face is that Congress is a crisis-oriented institution, with few mechanisms and little inclination to deal with problems before they become acute. . . . We need better distant early-warning signals, better mechanisms and institutional arrangements for handling problems which are not yet brush fires, but which are already smoldering and may well cause the conflagrations of the future.

> —*Edward M. Kennedy. Speech,*
> *April 30, 1979.*

Courts, Justice, and Law

Law is the strongest link between man and freedom.

> —*John F. Kennedy. Law Day*
> *proclamation, May 1, 1961.*

We are dedicated to the proposition that liberty and law are inseparable; that we truly believe social progress strengthens and enlarges freedom.

—*Robert F. Kennedy. Speech,*
Law Day Ceremonies of the
Virginia State Bar, Roanoke,
Virginia, May 1, 1962.

In our society, laws are administered to protect and expand individual freedom, not to compel individuals to follow the logic other men impose on them.

—*Robert F. Kennedy. Address,*
American Jewish Congress,
New York City, October 28,
1962.

Justice delayed is democracy denied.

—*Robert F. Kennedy.* The
Pursuit of Justice, *1964.*

If one man is denied equal protection under the law, we cannot be sure that we will enjoy freedom of speech or any other of our fundamental rights.

—*Robert F. Kennedy. Speech,*
June 21, 1961.

As far back as Justinian's Rome, criminal codes have been symbols of justice, examples of society's commitment to the principle of fairness. In this respect, the current federal criminal code is a disgrace. Congresses over the years have enacted some three thousand criminal laws, piling one on top of another, until we have a structure that looks more like a Rube Goldberg contraption than a comprehensive criminal code.

—*Edward M. Kennedy. Speech,*
January 19, 1978.

As long as a man is handicapped before the bar of justice because of his poverty, our task as lawyers is not done.

—Robert F. Kennedy. Address,
American Bar Association
House of Delegates, San
Francisco, August 6, 1962.

Legal services, particularly defense in criminal cases, are not like houses or automobiles where those with more money can buy better products without affecting the basic functioning of society. When one defendant cannot afford a complete defense, justice is being rationed.

—Robert F. Kennedy. Address,
American Bar Association
House of Delegates, San
Francisco, August 6, 1962.

The decision of the courts, however much we might disagree with them, in the final analysis must be followed and respected. If we disagree with a court decision and thereafter irresponsibly assail the court and defy its rulings, we challenge the foundations of our society.

—Robert F. Kennedy. Speech,
Law Day Exercises, University
of Georgia Law School,
May 6, 1961.

Whenever men take the law into their own hands, the loser is the law—and when the law loses, freedom languishes.

—Robert F. Kennedy. Address
before the Joint Defense
Appeal of the American
Jewish Committee and the
Anti-Defamation League of
B'nai B'rith, Chicago,
June 21, 1961.

Policy formation without public participation is like faith and hope without charity.

> —*Edward M. Kennedy. Speech,*
> *June 3, 1975.*

In a democratic society, law is the form which free men give to justice. The glory of justice and the majesty of law are created not just by the Constitution—nor the courts—nor by the officers of the law—nor by the lawyers—but by the men and women who constitute our society—who are the protectors of the law as they are themselves protected by the law. Justice, in short, is everybody's business.

> —*Robert F. Kennedy. Speech,*
> *Law Day Ceremonies of the*
> *Virginia State Bar, Roanoke,*
> *Virginia, May 1, 1962.*

In George Orwell's world of the future, the Ministry of Hate was called the Ministry of Love, and the Ministry of War was called the Ministry of Peace. It must be the purpose of government to ensure that the department over which I presided is more than a Department of Prosecution and is, in fact, the Department of Justice.

> —*Robert F. Kennedy, July 1964.*

John Adams in the original draft of the Massachusetts Constitution spoke of "a government of laws, and not of men." If the members of this Bar will forgive me, I fear that from time to time in our history we have tended to construe this as meaning a government of *lawyers* and not of men.

> —*Robert F. Kennedy. Speech,*
> *Law Day Ceremonies of the*
> *Virginia State Bar, Roanoke,*
> *Virginia, May 1, 1962.*

My biggest problem as counsel is to keep my temper. I think we all feel that when a witness comes before the United States Senate he has an obligation to speak frankly and tell the truth. To see people sit in front of us and lie and evade makes me boil inside. But you can't lose your temper—if you do, the witness has gotten the best of you.

—*Robert F. Kennedy. Notes for*
Life *close-up, 1957.*

Membership in the bar has special privileges—and special responsibilities. More lawyers need to give their time and talent to their communities, by providing pro bono legal services for the indigent. Equal justice under law is not just a phrase carved in marble. It is the essence of the law, and the continuing challenge for our times is to see that it is a reality in our lives.

—*Edward M. Kennedy. Speech,*
Judicial Conference of the
United States Court of Appeals
for the First Circuit, Copley
Plaza Hotel, Washington,
D.C., September 13, 1993.

Agencies, the Cabinet, and Advisers

If you take the wrong course, and on occasion I have, the president bears the burden of the responsibility quite rightly. The advisers move on to new advice.

—*John F. Kennedy. Television*
and radio interview, "Year-
end Conversation with the
President," Washington, D.C.,
December 17, 1962.

As the head of the Maritime Commission, Joseph Kennedy made a request to the Senate Appropriations Committee, unheard-of from the head of a federal agency, to not release funds:

Giving us cash might involve an obligation to spend it, and we're not going to do that until we know where we stand.

—*Quoted in the* New York
Times, *August 17, 1937.*

On the CIA, after the Bay of Pigs debacle:

I know that outfit, and I wouldn't pay them a hundred bucks a week. It's a lucky thing they were found out early; the best thing that could have happened, in fact.

—*Joseph P. Kennedy. Quoted in*
William Manchester, Portrait
of a President, *1962.*
Kennedy had served on a
civilian watchdog committee
during the Eisenhower
administration.

We have found [the executive branch] is full of honest and useful public servants—but their capacity to act decisively at the exact time action is needed has too often been muffled in the morass of committees, timidities, and fictitious theories which have created a growing gap between decision and execution, between planning and reality.

—*John F. Kennedy. State of the*
Union Address, January 30,
1961.

I don't think the intelligence reports are all that hot. Some days I get more out of the *New York Times.*

—*John F. Kennedy.*

All my life I've known better than to depend on the experts. How could I have been so stupid, to let them go ahead?

—*John F. Kennedy on the Bay*
of Pigs invasion.

You know how many people they employ there? Thousands! You know how many I get to appoint? Hundreds! Hell, they've got their own damned government over there. I'm not going to be able to change their thinking.

> —*John F. Kennedy on the State Department, in conversation with Senator George Smathers shortly after taking over the presidency.*

While trying to pick a secretary of state for the Kennedy administration, Robert Kennedy reflected on the importance of the selection:

The toughest and most important was the selection for Secretary of State. . . . I said in the last analysis Jack was going to be Secretary of State; this was a position in which he would be making his own decisions. All he needed was advice and ideas by an expert but the decisions would be made by him.

> —*Robert F. Kennedy. Memorandum, February 9, 1961.*

I don't care what it is, but if I need something fast, the CIA is the place I go.

> —*John F. Kennedy.*

The FBI didn't know anything, really, about these people who were the major gangsters in the United States. . . . That was rather a shock to me. . . . I sent the same request to the Bureau of Narcotics, and they had something on every one of them.

> —*Robert F. Kennedy. Remarks on his investigation of labor rackets. Interview for Oral History, November 4, 1964.*

They [the FBI] want the publicity from their press releases, but where they have a natural opportunity to get into these things [racketeering], particularly where it affects us, they are very reluctant to do so.

—*Robert F. Kennedy.*
Memorandum, May 29, 1958.

Bureaucracy

Government departments are like icebergs.

—*John F. Kennedy. Remark to*
Benjamin Bradlee, May 15,
1962.

When asked in an interview about his habit of calling departments personally, President Kennedy explained:

Yes, I still do that when I can, because I think there is a great tendency in government to have papers stay on desks too long, and it seems to me that is really one function. . . . After all, the president can't administer a department, but at least he can be a stimulant.

—*John F. Kennedy. Television*
and radio interview, "Year-
end Conversation with the
President," Washington, D.C.,
December 17, 1962.

Our large cities are totally impersonal, they crank human beings through their daily activities. Our large universities are totally impersonal, they stamp our people with fixed credentials. Our large industries are totally impersonal, they employ people in repetitive tasks empty of a sense of value. Our large units of government are totally impersonal, they exist for their own sake rather than for the people they serve. And all these institutions seem unresponsive to the individual complaint or desire. There is a general sense of helplessness, a feeling of uselessness.

—Edward M. Kennedy.
Acceptance speech for
nomination to senatorial
candidacy by the
Massachusetts Democratic
Convention, Amherst,
June 12, 1970.

For too long we have accepted a watchmaker's theory of the federal universe. Congress and the administration construct the programs and set them ticking—and then leave them running on their own for years or even decades.

—Edward M. Kennedy. Speech,
April 29, 1976.

Our lives and economy are increasingly caught up in an ever-constricting web of laws and regulations that threaten to bring our vaunted free-enterprise system to its knees unless we act.

The fall of the Ottoman Empire at the beginning of this century is widely attributed to the excesses of a top-heavy civil service and a system of administrative regulation imposed by a bureaucracy run wild.

The traditional American reaction to a problem or abuse has been to say, "There ought to be a law." But now, as we survey the complex legal framework of the nation, we should also be prepared to say of many areas, "There ought not to be a law."

—Edward M. Kennedy. Speech,
June 14, 1979.

The people of this country come first—not the institutions.

—Joseph P. Kennedy II.
Interview, May 7, 1989.

Campaigns

We're going to sell Jack like soap flakes.

> —*Joseph P. Kennedy on*
> *campaign strategy for John F.*
> *Kennedy.*

It's our money, and we're free to spend it any way we choose. It's part of this campaign business. If you have money, you spend it to win. And the more you can afford, the more you'll spend.

> —*Rose Kennedy on campaign*
> *financing. Quoted in Ralph G.*
> *Martin,* A Hero for Our Time,
> *1983.*

I just received the following wire from my generous daddy— "Dear Jack, don't buy a single vote more than is necessary. I'll be damned if I'm going to pay for a landslide."

> —*John F. Kennedy. Speech at*
> *the Gridiron Dinner,*
> *Washington, D.C., 1958.*

If there wasn't the promise of some reward, no one would ever contribute to a political campaign.

> —*John F. Kennedy. Remark*
> *during a conversation on the*
> *linguistic and diplomatic*
> *inexperience of most*
> *ambassadors.*

What have I got to lose besides Dad's money?

> —*Robert F. Kennedy,*
> *considering whether he should*
> *run for president, 1968.*

People say, "Kennedy bought the election. Kennedy could never have been elected if his father hadn't been a millionaire." Well, it wasn't the Kennedy name and the Kennedy money that won the election. I beat [Senator] Lodge because I hustled for three years. I worked for what I got.

—*John F. Kennedy. Quoted in Ralph G. Martin and Ed Plaut,* Front Runner, Dark Horse, *1960.*

Public financing of elections is the wisest possible investment that American taxpayers can make in the future of their country.

—*Edward M. Kennedy. Speech, May 5, 1977.*

Robert F. Kennedy's first campaign speech was given during John Kennedy's 1952 campaign for the seat of Senator Cabot Lodge. An appearance by a Kennedy had been promised, but no one was able to make it. Robert, more accustomed to "back room" politics, stepped forward and gave his first campaign speech, quoted here in its entirety:

My brother Jack couldn't be here. My mother couldn't be here. My sister Eunice couldn't be here. My sister Jean couldn't be here. But if my brother Jack were here, he'd tell you Lodge has a very bad voting record. Thank you.

We couldn't win relying on the Democratic political machine, so we had to build our own machine.

—*Robert F. Kennedy. Remark on Jack's 1952 Senate campaign in a interview.*

If you win, the reporters will always write about well-oiled machines and super-planning. If you lose, they will always write about hopeless incompetence. I have a simple theory: that campaigns come to an absolute end within a given time; that you can recruit good people and ask them to do a lot of things in that brief period; that some things work and some

won't; that, if something is not working, change it, and be
prepared to change it again; and that out of all the activity a
momentum will develop which will carry you through.

> —*Robert F. Kennedy. Remark to
> colleague Arthur
> Schlesinger Jr., 1964.*

The efficiency with which it [the 1960 presidential campaign]
is run—the amazing results it achieves—all because it is first
a purely family team at the center. Jack, his brothers, his
brothers-in-law, and the overall strategy of their father, who
I doubt will ever get credit for the constant, unremitting labor
day and night which he had devoted to making his son
President.

> —*Rose Kennedy. Journal entry,
> June 23, 1960.*

I could get in trouble for doing that [talking about politics].
I don't know enough about the issues. I think I'll just answer
questions about the family.

> —*Jean Kennedy Smith.
> Interview on the presidential
> campaign,* Washington Star,
> *February 26, 1960.*

Jack liked to have a female member of the family with him.
I think it was probably pretty smart politics to have a female
member of the family standing close right next to him because
there were a lot of other women that wanted to stand right
next to him and this looked better.

> —*Joan Kennedy. Comment on
> the 1960 presidential
> campaign, quoted in Leamer,*
> The Kennedy Women, *1994.*

The office the President of the United States is the greatest and the most important in the world. And yet . . . do you realize that to get the nomination for that office candidates have the worst organizations. That's because good men—men who have important jobs—don't want to give up their jobs to work for a candidate before he gets the nomination, because it's too risky. He may not get it, and then where are they? And the others—the ones you *can* hire, the ones who are available—aren't any good and you can't build an organization with them anyhow.

> —*Joseph P. Kennedy. Reflections on his son's presidential campaign. Quoted in Ralph G. Martin and Ed Plaut,* Front Runner, Dark Horse, *1960.*

On his role in his son's campaign:

Well, I just call people. You call people that you know and ask them to help in any way they can. . . . I've made a lot of contacts all over the country. You just ask them to help. That's all.

> —*Joseph P. Kennedy. Quoted in Ralph G. Martin and Ed Plaut,* Front Runner, Dark Horse, *1960.*

When asked if Jack's early lead was too much too soon:

The only way we can win this is to wrap it up very, very early. In our position, that's the risk we're most willing to take, and it's the least of our worries. When you start from scratch, you've got to run like the dickens all the way.

> —*Joseph P. Kennedy. Interview,* Time, *May 5, 1958.*

In 1960, when a Democratic politician mentioned that Jack was a bit young for the presidency:

He is, but I'm seventy-two and I want to be around to enjoy it.

—*Joseph P. Kennedy. Quoted in
the* New York Herald-Tribune,
November 23, 1963.

After Jack won all seven primaries he had entered:

For the Kennedys, it's either the outhouse or the castle—no in-between.

—*Joseph P. Kennedy. Remark to
a friend, 1960. Quoted in
Richard J. Whalen,* The
Founding Father: The Story of
Joseph Kennedy, *1964.*

Early in the campaign, the suggestion arose that Kennedy could become Johnson's running mate.

It's first place or nothing. Not for chalk, money, or marbles will we take second place. Nobody's going to make a deal with us in a back room somewhere for a second place on the ticket.

—*John F. Kennedy. Quoted in*
Time, *July 11, 1960.*

In a typically roughshod manner, Robert Kennedy silenced fractional fighting in the Democratic party:

Gentlemen, I don't give a damn if the state and county organizations survive after November, and I don't give a damn if *you* survive. I want to elect John F. Kennedy.

—*Robert F. Kennedy. Remark,
1960. Quoted in Robert E.
Thompson and Hortense
Myers,* Robert F. Kennedy:
The Brother Within, *1962.*

Campaign strategy for West Virginia, not in 1960 known for tolerance of Catholics:

It is simply food, family, and flag in southern West Virginia.

> —*Robert F. Kennedy.*
> *Statements in campaign*
> *strategy meeting, April*
> *8, 1960.*

So young and so wrong.

> —*John F. Kennedy, upon seeing*
> *a young girl with a Nixon*
> *sign, Mt. Prospect,*
> *Illinois, 1960.*

Do you realize the responsibility I carry? I'm the only person between Nixon and the White House.

> —*John F. Kennedy. Remark to a*
> *supporter during the 1960*
> *campaign. Quoted in Theodore*
> *C. Sorensen,* Kennedy, *1965.*

On the Right Track with Jack.

> —*Democratic presidential*
> *campaign slogan for John F.*
> *Kennedy, 1960.*

You have in your grasp the opportunity to nominate the next president of the United States. Such support can never be forgotten by the president.

> —*Edward M. Kennedy,*
> *campaigning for John F.*
> *Kennedy in Wyoming, 1960.*

Somewhat to my own surprise, I found myself turning into a regular "politician." I didn't miss a chance to ask anyone to vote for Jack. I talked with taxi drivers, elevator operators, waitresses, porters, manicurists, and anyone with whom I could strike up a conversation.

—*Rose F. Kennedy.* Times to
Remember, *1974.*

As our population increases, as the problems of our society become more complex, and as the cost of political campaigns continues to mount—it becomes more and more clear that the package is more important than the product; that the perceived "image" of a candidate is often more important than what he says. . . . In the state that brought moviemaking to a high art, this has produced the new phenomenon of the actor as candidate—and a successful candidate at that. . . . The cost of campaigning has become so high that to make a candidate and his views well enough known in a state like California or New York is impossible without either a well-known personality or large sums of money.

As an unknown with virtually no funds, I was, of course, an exception.

—*Robert F. Kennedy. Speech,
Skidmore College,
February 22, 1967.*

Let's face it. I appeal best to people who have problems.

—*Robert F. Kennedy. Remark
made during the Oregon
primaries, 1968. He lost the
primary in that state.*

A frequent story about a meeting with a mother superior at one of his campaign stops:

She said she had been praying to Saint Jude for me. I thanked her—then asked somebody who Saint Jude was. I learned he is the patron saint of lost causes.

—*Robert F. Kennedy, 1968.*

When reporters asked Robert Kennedy in 1968 what he thought of a Johnson-Kennedy ticket, he replied:

I'd be willing, but I'm not sure that Mr. Johnson would accept the vice presidency.

To the question of his response to an alleged offer from Johnson for the VP spot:

I explained to him that I thought a coalition government is possible in Saigon—but not here.
> —*Robert F. Kennedy, May 1968.*

For God's sake, Jackie, this could cost me five states.
> —*Robert F. Kennedy to Jacqueline Kennedy, after she told him her plans to marry Aristotle Onassis, 1968.*

I know not everybody thinks I'm a very strong candidate. But there are some who think I can win. George Hamilton called last night and asked me for my daughter's telephone number.
> —*Robert F. Kennedy. Campaign speech, Alabama, June 16, 1968.*

Well, I learned to lose, and for a Kennedy, that's hard.
> —*Edward M. Kennedy. Response to the question of what he had learned from his failed bid for the Democratic presidential nomination, 1980.*

Polls have become the quintessential pseudo-events of the preprimary campaign.
> —*Edward M. Kennedy.*

Speak of a vision, work hard, and get a good road map of Iowa.

> —*Edward M. Kennedy, giving*
> *advice to presidential primary*
> *candidates. Quoted in*
> Newsweek, *July 13, 1987.*

Debate, Rhetoric, and Discussion

It is much easier to make the speeches than to finally make the judgments.

> —*John F. Kennedy. Interview,*
> *1962.*

Senator, we're speaking English, but we're not talking the same language.

> —*Robert F. Kennedy. To*
> *Senator Sam Ervin. Quoted on*
> PBS, *Senator Sam,*
> *October 25, 1988.*

Attempting to deliver a speech to a gathering of Cesar Chávez's United Farm Workers in Spanish, using a phonetic translation, Robert Kennedy realized the Spanish tongue was not his forte:

I'm murdering the language, Cesar, is that right?

Chávez agreed with a smile and nod, and Kennedy continued in English.

An exchange between JFK and his sister Eunice during his administration, when she gave frequent speeches relating to her role as consultant to the President's Panel on Mental Retardation.

EUNICE: You should put more fire into your speeches.
JOHN: And you should put more of your speeches into the fire.

In 1966 the Senate held hearings on auto safety, and Ralph Nader was called to testify. Senator Carl Curtis, however, made a point of interrupting his statement. Robert F. Kennedy asked him if Nader could finish, and the following exchange ensued:

CURTIS: I have no objection to his reading his statement.

KENNEDY: Then maybe we would understand his position. . . . First, you admit you haven't read the book; and secondly, you haven't heard his testimony. Why don't you listen to his testimony and then criticize?

CURTIS: I have no objection to hearing his testimony, but when he loses me with—

KENNEDY: With big words?

Facts are what the country needs, not slogans. . . . The people who must suffer and give up their lives are entitled to know all the facts before their judgment can be won to the interventionist cause. It is a mockery of liberty to withhold from a democratic people the essential facts upon which this, the most awful decision of our times, must be based. We must have the completest candor; we must have the fullest disclosure; we must have the freest debate.

> —*Joseph P. Kennedy. Speech, Oglethorpe University, May 1941.*

Full and informing debate rests upon moderation and mutual indulgence. Men must seek acceptance of their views through reason, and not through intimidation; through argument, and not through accusation. We are all patriots here. We are all defenders of freedom. We are all Americans. To attack the motives of those who express concern about our present course—to challenge their very right to speak freely—is to strike at the foundations of the democratic process which our fellow citizens, even today, are dying in order to protect.

> —*Robert F. Kennedy. Statement on Vietnam protests, February 19, 1966.*

The intolerant man will not rely on persuasion, or on the worth of the idea. He would deny to others the very freedom of opinion or of dissent which he so stridently demands for himself. He cannot trust democracy.

> —Robert F. Kennedy. Speech, dedication of the John F. Kennedy Interfaith Chapel, West Georgia College, Carrollton, Georgia, May 26, 1964.

The words which submerge us, all too often, speak the language of a day irrelevant to our young. And the language of politics is too often insincerity—which we have perhaps too easily accepted, but to the young it is particularly offensive. George Orwell wrote a generation ago that "in our time, political speech and writing are largely the defense of the indefensible. . . . Political language has to consist largely of euphemism, question-begging, and sheer cloudy vagueness." There is too much truth for comfort in that statement today.

> —Robert F. Kennedy. Speech, Americans for Democratic Action dinner, Philadelphia, February 24, 1967.

Too often in recent years, we have allowed debates on major issues to be polarized beyond the point of no return. We cannot afford to let bad debate drive out the good.

> —Edward M. Kennedy. Speech, November 2, 1975.

Political Parties

We observe today not a victory of party, but a celebration of freedom—symbolizing an end, as well as a beginning—signifying renewal, as well as change.

> —John F. Kennedy. Inaugural address, January 20, 1961.

Well, I don't call myself anything except a Democrat who's been elected president of the United States, and I hope I am a responsible president.

> —*John F. Kennedy. Response to the question asking for a definition of his political philosophy, press conference, February 1, 1961.*

Our duty as a party is not to our party alone, but to the nation and, indeed, to all mankind. Our duty is not merely the preservation of political power but the preservation of peace and freedom.

> —*John F. Kennedy. Undelivered speech, Dallas, Texas, November 22, 1963.*

Both major parties today seek to serve the national interest.

> —*John F. Kennedy.*

Parties are instruments of government. . . . The business of parties is not just to win elections. It is to govern. And a party cannot govern if it is disunited.

> —*Robert F. Kennedy. Speech, Kings County Democratic Party dinner, Brooklyn, New York, May 20, 1965.*

They are not going to vote for the Democratic party because things are fine or because they "never had it so good." They are not going to pull the Democratic lever because they want to "stand pat" or "keep cool." They will not favor our cause if they want to keep the status quo or stand in the way of change or go back to days that are gone. For if this is the course they wish, there is another party, the Republican party, which is far better qualified, by history, tradition, and temperament, to preside over stagnation and drift.

—Robert F. Kennedy. Speech,
Democratic State Dinner,
Columbus, Ohio, October 8,
1966.

I think that when we sign up for the Democratic party, we don't say that we are never going to disagree. I think that there is much to disagree about.

—Robert F. Kennedy.
Appearance on Face the
Nation, November 26, 1967.

The most troublesome questions confronting Americans do not have Republican answers or Democratic answers. . . . They have human answers, and American answers, for they are the questions that ask what kind of life we want to lead and what kind of nation we want to have.

—Edward M. Kennedy.
Commencement address,
Manhattanville College,
June 12, 1970.

I come here as a Democrat. I reject such qualifiers as New Democrat or Old Democrat or Neo Democrat. I am committed to the enduring principles of the Democratic party, and I am proud of its great tradition of service to the people who are the heart and strength of this nation—working families and the middle class. . . .

If Democrats run for cover, if we become pale carbon copies of the opposition and try to act like Republicans, we will lose—and deserve to lose. . . . Democrats must be more than warmed-over Republicans. The last thing this country needs is two Republican parties.

—Edward M. Kennedy. Speech,
National Press Club,
Washington, D.C., January 11,
1995. The Democrats had just
lost the majority in Congress.

The new Republican majority in Congress is trying to turn back the clock on decades of bipartisan progress we've made together. Well, with priorities like that, they won't stay a majority very long!

> —*Edward M. Kennedy. Speech,*
> *American Federation of*
> *Teachers Legislative Congress,*
> *Washington, D.C., September*
> *20, 1995.*

National conventions . . . continue to play a vital role in American political life. . . . Our political parties consist of competing and sometimes conflicting interests that are forced to find common ground. And while it's easy to be cynical about all the flag waving and political rhetoric, in the end conventions provide an institutional device for fulfilling our national motto, *E pluribus unum*—from many, one.

> —*John F. Kennedy Jr. Editor's*
> *letter,* George, *August 1996.*

Public Opinion

You must remember—it's not what you are that counts, but what people think you are.

> —*Joseph P. Kennedy to Eunice*
> *Kennedy when she asked,*
> *"Do you really think Jack can*
> *be a congressman?"*

The basis of effective government is public confidence.

> —*John F. Kennedy. Message to*
> *Congress, April 27, 1961.*

The worse I do, the more popular I get.

> —*John F. Kennedy, on how,*
> *after the Bay of Pigs fiasco,*
> *his approval rating was 82*
> *percent, higher than ever*
> *before. Quoted in*
> *Wallechinsky and Wallace,*
> The People's Almanac, *1975.*

One fifth of the people are against everything all the time.

> —*Robert F. Kennedy, 1964.*

There are times when we are more popular than others. If you are going into this kind of work for the reward at the polls, you could end up very disappointed. There are other reasons. You have to do it because you think it is the right thing to do, because you get some sense of satisfaction.

> —*Joseph P. Kennedy II. Quoted*
> *in the* Boston Globe
> Magazine, *May 23, 1993.*

Taxes and the Federal Budget

We had a taxpayers' revolution two hundred years ago, and we need another one today.

> —*Edward M. Kennedy. Speech,*
> *February 26, 1977.*

The aim of tax reform is not to plow up the whole garden, but to get rid of the weeds so that we can let the flowers grow.

> —*Edward M. Kennedy. Speech,*
> *July 1, 1977.*

If we are going to balance the federal budget, let us resolve that the burden will be shared by all—not just the cities, not just the poor and the black and the sick—so that no citizen pays too high a price for the cutbacks the future may have in store.

—*Edward M. Kennedy. Speech, June 19, 1978.*

People want an end to loopholes in the tax laws, so that those who eat at the most expensive restaurants will pay their way themselves, instead of making the Treasury foot the bill through tax deductions that are nothing more than food stamps for the rich.

—*Edward M. Kennedy. Speech, September 30, 1978.*

It is imperative that the Republicans end the shutdown of government. . . . All members of Congress should automatically have their pay withheld from them during such periods of crisis.

—*Patrick J. Kennedy. Press release, January 4, 1996, during a budget impasse.*

It does not take a constitutional amendment to reduce the federal deficit or balance the federal budget. All it takes is enough courage by Congress and the administration to make the tough decisions we're elected to make. If we're not willing to balance the budget, the Constitution can't do it for us.

—*Edward M. Kennedy. Statement opposing the Balanced Budget Amendment, March 1, 1994.*

Instead of devoting the time and effort to craft a responsible budget, the Republican majority asks us to amend the Constitution now, ask questions later. But the Constitution has served this nation through wars, economic depressions, and other crises far worse than the current budget deficit. Amending the Constitution should be the considered option of last resort, not the expedient course of first resort.

—*Edward M. Kennedy. Senate speech on the proposed Balanced Budget Amendment, February 7, 1995.*

We all want to balance the budget. But it cannot and should not be balanced on the backs of America's children. Enough is enough. Enough of back-room deals with high-paid corporate lobbyists. Enough of dismantling commitments made to children and families who need help the most. This debate is not about arcane economic theories—but about saving real children.

—*Edward M. Kennedy. Statement on Republican budget proposals, December 5, 1995.*

The old way of the government's taxing and spending just won't work any longer.

—*Joseph P. Kennedy II. Quoted in* U.S. News and World Report *profile, December 16, 1985.*

Education

I didn't know anything when I got out of college.

—*Robert F. Kennedy. Quoted in R. E. Thompson and Hortense Myers,* Robert F. Kennedy: The Brother Within, *1962.*

Of all the boys, Jack likes Harvard best. Bobby and Teddy don't care for it, and I guess I have the old Boston prejudice against it.

> —*Joseph P. Kennedy. Remark.*

The President was most fond of school. Can I ask you to do a favor for him? Stay in school, study as long as you can, and then work for your city and for Brazil.

> —*Robert F. Kennedy to a group of children at a community center named after Jack in Brazil. Quoted in the* New York Times, *November 23, 1965.*

Plato said that if we are to have any hope for the future, that those who have lanterns will pass them on to others. You must use your lamps, the lamps of your learning, to show our people past the forest of stereotypes and slogans into the clear light of reality and of fact and of truth.

> —*Robert F. Kennedy. Speech, University of Mississippi Law School Forum, Oxford, Mississippi, March 18, 1966.*

I can get a much better education outside of school. We Kennedys belong in the real world. That's where we function best.

> —*Joseph P. Kennedy II. Remark to a friend, 1972.*

I believe the time has already come when the first two years of college—just like elementary school or high school—should be free to all qualified students.

> —*Robert F. Kennedy. Speech, Sioux City, October 9, 1966.*

In this mobile society, with most Americans moving across state lines at least once in their lifetime, the education of a child in Iowa contributes to the whole nation—and a stunted education elsewhere can force Iowa to spend more on welfare and police and housing. Education is a national resource; it should be paid for on a national basis, with each paying his share as a citizen of the nation.

—Robert F. Kennedy. Speech,
Des Moines, Iowa.

It might be said now that I have the best of both worlds: a Harvard education and a Yale degree.

—John F. Kennedy. On being
awarded an honorary degree,
Yale Commencement Address,
June 11, 1962.

Many of the problems that we see in our educational programs today are a direct result of our delay in responding to our rapidly changing society. In the generation of our fathers and grandfathers, schools were expected to produce only a few leaders. Their principal output was unskilled workers. During that era, managers and professionals were all too often members of an elite class. The fantastically rapid development of modern technology has changed all that. The call of new opportunity has gone out to millions of American youth, and our education system must respond.

—Edward M. Kennedy. Speech,
First Northeast Regional
Conference of the National
Council for Social Studies,
April 11, 1970.

If there are some children in this land—whether because they are black or because they were born on a reservation or because they speak a different language or because they are poor—if there are some children who do not have an equal opportunity for a quality education, then there are some children who are not free.

> —Edward M. Kennedy. Speech,
> April 25, 1977.

The Republican cuts are real, and the Republican contingency add-backs are a sham. Education is not a contingency for the American people—it is a necessity, and Congress should act accordingly.

> —Edward M. Kennedy. Senate
> speech on the proposed
> Republican budget, March 7,
> 1996.

How ironic it is that many of the same individuals who are fighting to repeal federal support for higher education are also fighting to repeal the assault weapons ban and make those deadly weapons available on the streets and neighborhoods of cities across America. Do they think we have too many college students in our communities, but not enough guns? We have often heard that the pen is mightier than the sword. I guess they now feel that the pen is more dangerous than a semiautomatic machine gun.

> —Edward M. Kennedy.
> Statement to The College
> Democrats of America, 1995.

The Military

It is an unfortunate fact that we can secure peace only by preparing for war.

> —John F. Kennedy. Campaign
> speech, Seattle, Washington,
> September 6, 1960.

We dare not tempt them with weakness. For only when our arms are sufficient beyond doubt can we be certain beyond doubt that they will never be employed.

—*John F. Kennedy. Inaugural address, January 20, 1961.*

To graduates of the Naval Academy:

You must know something about strategy and tactics and logic—logistics, but also economics and politics and diplomacy and history. You must know everything you can know about military power, and you must also understand the limits of military power. You must understand that few of the important problems of our time have, in the final analysis, been finally solved by military power alone.

—*John F. Kennedy. Commencement Address, United States Naval Academy, Annapolis, Maryland, June 7, 1961.*

There is no priority for this nation higher than guaranteeing our national security and safety. Without an effective military force, and without a worldwide understanding that we have the unwavering will to use this force when our national interests are in danger, we unnecessarily place our way of life in peril.

—*Edward M. Kennedy. Speech, June 3, 1969.*

The armed services continue to be a critical and worthwhile career for America's young men and women. If anything, it is now even more important for people of high caliber, committed to the nation's future, to serve in the armed forces.

—*Edward M. Kennedy. Speech, February 17, 1975.*

Over the years, an understanding of what America really stands for is going to count far more than missiles, aircraft carriers, and supersonic bombers. The big changes of the future will result from this understanding or lack of it.

—*Robert F. Kennedy. Speech, 1964.*

With the irony of a paradoxical world, the surest guarantee of peace at present is the power to wage war. The United States has that power. It comes from our programs of strength and deterrence. Without this strength we could not have achieved the truly momentous victory of the 1962 Cuban missile crisis. Without this strength we cannot reasonably expect to achieve other objectives even at the conference table in our constant pursuit of peace.

—*Robert F. Kennedy. Speech, 1964.*

When an insurgent uprising threatened to unseat Jerome Bonaparte, his brother Napoleon told him "use your bayonets." Jerome replied, "Brother, you can do anything with bayonets—except sit on them." That is also true of more advanced weapons. Guns and bombs cannot fill empty stomachs or educate children, cannot build homes or heal the sick. But these are the ends for which men establish and obey governments; they will give their allegiance only to governments that meet these needs.

—*Robert F. Kennedy.* To Seek a Newer World, *1967.*

The city of Hiroshima stands as more than a monument to massive death and destruction. It stands as a living testament to the necessity for progress toward nuclear disarmament.

—*Edward M. Kennedy. Speech, January 11, 1978.*

Never again should black rain fall.

*—Edward M. Kennedy. Speech
on nuclear disarmament,
January 30, 1978.*

The sad reality is that the course, the pace, and the objectives of arms control policies have been more influenced by the arms producers than by the arms controllers.

*—Edward M. Kennedy. Speech,
December 2, 1975.*

By any measure, the United States is far and away the world's chief arms merchant.

*—Edward M. Kennedy. Speech,
December 4, 1975.*

It makes no sense to sacrifice real and verifiable reductions in the Russian nuclear arsenal, in exchange for a multibillion-dollar national missile defense that will leave us less secure. A decade ago, we should have left Star Wars in Hollywood where it belonged—and that's where this senseless sequel belongs too.

*—Edward M. Kennedy.
Statement opposing the
proposed unilateral
abrogation of the Anti-
Ballistic Missile Treaty, signed
in 1972, 1995.*

Science and Technology

You yourself said to Khrushchev, "You may be ahead of us in rocket thrust, but we're ahead of you in color television." I think that color television is not as important as rocket thrust.

—John F. Kennedy, in presidential debate with Richard M. Nixon, 1960.

Let both sides seek to invoke the wonders of science instead of its terrors. Together let us explore the stars, conquer the deserts, eradicate disease, tap the ocean depths, and encourage the arts and commerce.

—John F. Kennedy. Inaugural address, January 20, 1961.

We are very concerned that we do not put a man in space in order to gain some additional prestige and have a man take disproportional risk, so we are going to be extremely careful in our work, and even if we come in second in putting a man in space, I will still be satisfied if when we finally do put a man in space, his chances of survival are as high as I think they must be.

—John F. Kennedy. Press conference, February 8, 1961.

In a very real sense, it will not be one man going to the moon—if we make this judgment affirmatively, it will be an entire nation. For all of us must work to put him there.

—John F. Kennedy. Special message to Congress on Urgent National Needs, May 25, 1961.

We believe that if men have the talent to invent new machines that put men out of work, they have the talent to put those men back to work.

> —*John F. Kennedy. Speech,*
> *Wheeling, West Virginia,*
> *September 27, 1962.*

Properly used technology should not displace workers, but should speed them on their way to new jobs more quickly.

> —*Robert F. Kennedy. Senate*
> *speech, June 28, 1966.*

Man is still the most extraordinary computer of all.

> —*John F. Kennedy. Speech, May*
> *21, 1963.*

·5·

The World

at Large

Environment

The supreme reality of our time is the vulnerability of this planet.

—*John F. Kennedy. Speech,*
Dublin, Ireland, June 28,
1963.

On a trip to Latin America last year, I saw people in Recife, in the poorest part of Brazil, who ate crabs which lived off the garbage that the people themselves threw in the shallow water near their shabby homes. And whenever I tell this story to Americans, the reaction is: how sad; how terrible; that such poverty, such underdevelopment, should exist in the world. But we New Yorkers are in a poor position from which to extend pity. For every year the average New Yorker—old and young, rich and poor, athlete or infirm recluse—breathes in 750 pounds of his own wastes.

—*Robert F. Kennedy. Statement,*
New York–New Jersey
Metropolitan Air Pollution
Control Conference, January 4,
1967.

People are beginning to realize that we are a part of nature, not outside it. We are beginning to understand that instead of conquering nature, we must live in harmony with it.

—*Edward M. Kennedy. Speech,*
January 3, 1970.

We face the alarming possibility that among the enormous number of substances that our highly industrialized society is spewing into the environment are some that even now may be causing massive cancer epidemics for the next generation of Americans. We are in the impossible position of walking through a minefield blindfolded, with the knowledge that the devices we trigger today may not explode until our children walk through that field a generation from now.

> —*Edward M. Kennedy. Speech, February 15, 1978.*

War and Peace

Mankind must put an end to war or war will put an end to mankind.

> —*John F. Kennedy in a speech to the UN General Assembly, September 25, 1961.*

I am pro-peace. I pray, hope, and work for peace.

> —*Joseph P. Kennedy. Remarks to reporters. Quoted in the* New York Times, *December 15, 1938.*

The party is on.

> —*Joseph P. Kennedy. Remark to U.S. Secretary of State Cordell Hull after Germany invaded Poland, August 27, 1939.*

It's the end of the world, the end of everything.

> —*Joseph P. Kennedy to President Roosevelt, after informing him that England would declare war on Germany the next morning, September 1, 1939.*

You had the feeling of an era ending, and everyone had a very good time at the end.

> —*Joseph P. Kennedy. Remarks on the shopping sprees and parties of the English as World War II came closer, during British negotiations with Hitler over Czechoslovakia, September 1938.*

Today, individual, brooding silence was general, as were unsmiling, unemotional faces. Everyone unutterably shocked and depressed, feeling from the Prime Minister's talk that his hopes for peace are shattered and that war is inevitable.

> —*Rose F. Kennedy. Journal entry, September 27, 1938.*

The death and destruction of everything we stand for is inevitable.

> —*Joseph P. Kennedy. Interview with* Collier's, *November 26, 1940.*

Keep praying for civilization because heaven knows it needs it.

> —*Joseph P. Kennedy. Letter to Eunice Kennedy, September 11, 1940.*

I have yet to talk to any military or naval expert of any nationality this week who thinks that, with the present and prospective set-up of England and France on one side and Germany and Russia and their potential allies on the other, England has a Chinaman's chance. . . . England and France can't quit, whether they would like to or not, and I am convinced, because I live here, that England will go down fighting.

Unfortunately, I am one who does not believe that is going to do the slightest bit of good in this case.

> —*Joseph P. Kennedy. Letter to President Roosevelt, September 1939.*

As you love America, don't let anything that comes out of any country in the world make you believe you can make a situation one whit better by getting into war. There is no place in this fight for us. It's going to be bad enough as it is.

> —*Joseph P. Kennedy on America's involvement in World War II. Speech, Boston, Massachusetts, December 9, 1939.*

I hope when you grow up you will dedicate your life to trying to make people happy instead of making them miserable, as war does.

> —*Joseph P. Kennedy. Letter to Edward M. Kennedy during the London blitz.*

During a lull in battle—a Jap parachuted into the water. We went to pick him up as he floated along—and got within about 20 yards of him. He suddenly threw aside his life jacket and pulled out a revolver and fired two shots at our bridge. I had been praising the Lord and passing the ammunition right alongside—but that slowed me up a bit—the thought of him sitting in the water—battling an entire ship.

> —*John F. Kennedy. Letter to Lem Billings, May 6, 1943.*

An Americans energy's are divided. He wants to kill but he is also trying desperately to prevent himself from being killed.

> —*John F. Kennedy. Letter to Inga Arvad, September 26, 1943.*

When I read that we will fight the Japs for years if necessary, and will sacrifice hundreds of thousands if we must—I always like to check from where he is talking—it's seldom out here. People get so used to talking about billions of dollars and millions of soldiers that thousands of dead sounds like a drip in the bucket. But if those thousands want to live as much as the ten I saw [the ten American sailors he was stranded with on a Japanese island for six days]—they should measure their words with great, great care.

—John F. Kennedy, in a letter to his father, received September 12, 1943.

On the presidential coat of arms, the American eagle holds in his right talon the olive branch, while in his left he holds a bundle of arrows. We intend to give equal attention to both.

—John F. Kennedy. State of the Union Address, January 30, 1961.

[We are faced with] another kind of war—new in its intensity, ancient in its origins—war by guerrillas, subversives, insurgents, assassins; war by ambush instead of by combat; by infiltration instead of aggression; seeking victory by eroding and exhausting the enemy instead of engaging him.

—John F. Kennedy, 1961.

Twice within the memory of living men . . . the most advanced and cultured societies of the world have torn themselves and each other apart for causes so slight, in relation to the cost of the struggle, that it is impossible to regard them as other than excuses for the expression of some darker impulse.

—Robert F. Kennedy. To Seek a Newer World, *1967.*

I speak of peace . . . as the necessary rational end of rational men. I realize that the pursuit of peace is not as dramatic as the pursuit of war—and frequently the words of the pursuer fall on deaf ears. But we have no more urgent task. . . .

The United States, as the world knows, will never start a war. We do not want a war. We do not now expect a war. This generation of Americans has already had enough—more than enough—of war and hate and oppression. We shall be prepared if others wish it. We shall be alert to try to stop it. But we shall also do our part to build a world of peace where the weak are safe and the strong are just.

> —*John F. Kennedy. Speech, American University, June 10, 1963.*

P eace does not come automatically from a "peace treaty."

> —*John F. Kennedy. Press conference, Washington, D.C., July 19, 1961.*

T he mere absence of war is not peace.

> —*John F. Kennedy. State of the Union Address, January 14, 1963.*

A nuclear disaster, spread by winds and waters and fear, could well engulf the great and the small, the rich and the poor, the committed and the uncommitted alike.

> —*John F. Kennedy.*

A s we seek to improve the world in which we live and to secure its people against the scourge of war and want, we must understand that peace is not a final victory, but a continual effort.

> —*Edward M. Kennedy. Speech, December 2, 1975.*

The Cold War and Communism

The communists are interested in the welfare of the people. They take more interest in them than under the capitalistic system. They share with each other so that nobody is really poor. Dad doesn't know much about it, but I think it's great.

> —*Joseph P. Kennedy Jr., upon returning from England, c. 1936.*

Rose Kennedy on her visit to the Soviet Union in 1936:

Although there were many things that I saw that dismayed me—one which I need only mention, without elaboration, being the official doctrine of atheism—I did see why the Soviet system could be acceptable to the people of the U.S.S.R.; moreover, that many of its aims, if not many of the methods, were worthy of respect and discussion and study in some of our Western societies.

> —*Rose Kennedy.* Times to Remember, *1974.*

Russia does not want a major war now or in the near future. . . . The basic world policy for the U.S. should be to prevent World War III.

> —*Joseph P. Kennedy. Article,* Life, *March 1946.*

Permit communism to have its trial outside the Soviet Union if that shall be the fate or will of certain people. In most of these countries a few years will demonstrate the inability of communism to achieve its promises, while through this period the disillusioned experimenters will be observing the benefits of the American way of life, and most of them will emulate it. . . . The dangers at home are far more real to me.

> —*Joseph P. Kennedy. Interview, the* New York Times, *March 21, 1947.*

I insist that, when public officials advocate the policy of underwriting the salvation of the rest of the world from communism, they are morally bound to show the American people just where the money can come from—out of the pocket of the American taxpayer.

> —*Joseph P. Kennedy. Quoted in the* Boston Sunday Advertiser, *May 25, 1947.*

If portions of Europe or Asia wish to go communistic or even to have communism thrust upon them, we cannot stop it. Instead we must make sure of our strength and be certain not to fritter it away in battles that could not be won. . . . We can do well to mind our own business and interfere only when somebody threatens our business and our homes.

> —*Joseph P. Kennedy, on the Truman Doctrine, 1947.*

The seeds that make for communism in Europe are too deep to be reached by a recovery plan.

> —*Joseph P. Kennedy. Comment on the Marshall Plan, unpublished article, spring 1948.*

We should still fight to prevent Europe and Asia from becoming dominated by one great military power, and we will oppose bitterly, I believe, the suffering people of Europe and Asia from succumbing to the soporific ideology of Red totalitarianism.

> —*John F. Kennedy, taking direct issue with his father's statements in his first House speech on foreign policy, April 1, 1947.*

No matter what we try to do, 145 million people cannot reform, police, and feed the globe. Russia cannot do it either. No nation that has sought to assume that burden has been able to stand the strain. And the atom bomb will not alter that basic fact, for wars as such solve nothing.

> —*Joseph P. Kennedy. Draft of an unpublished article, spring 1948.*

Communism thrives on static discontent as sin thrives on idleness.

> —*Robert F. Kennedy. Article, Boston Post, June 6, 1948.*

The truth is that our only real hope is to keep Russia, if she chooses to march, on the other side of the Atlantic, and make communism much too costly for her to try and cross the seas. It may be that Europe for a decade or a generation or more will turn communistic. But in doing so, it may break off itself as a united force. Communism still has to prove itself to its peoples as a government that will achieve for them a better way of living. The more people that it will have to govern, the more necessary it becomes for those who govern to justify themselves to those being governed. The more peoples that are under its yoke, the greater are the possibilities of revolt.

> —*Joseph P. Kennedy. Speech, University of Virginia, December 1950.*

Why should they take risks they don't have to? . . . Stalin is an old man, and old men are traditionally cautious.

> —*John F. Kennedy, commenting on the Soviet threat to Western Europe before the Senate Foreign Relations Committee, February 22, 1951.*

There is a strong liberal feeling throughout Europe that is a valuable asset in the fight against communism. By terming this as a communistic movement we are only convincing the people over there that we are driving them into a war.

—*Joseph P. Kennedy. Interview, North American Newspaper Alliance, May 20, 1951.*

Communism cannot be met effectively merely by force of arms.

—*John F. Kennedy. Radio address, November 14, 1951.*

Must give the same aura to democracy. . . . We only have status quo to offer these people. Commies can offer a change.

—*Robert F. Kennedy. Journal entry recording and commenting on Indian Prime Minister Jawaharlal Nehru's remark over dinner that communism had appeal to developing countries because it was associated with ideas that are "worth dying for," October 1951.*

If we adopt a policy of intervention, a strong temptation is presented to those in power to picture all opposition forces as communistic in order to gain American aid, remain in control and incidentally save their own lives. The United States if it wishes to keep its friends in Asia cannot afford to be duped.

—*Robert F. Kennedy. Article written for the* Boston Post, *September 8, 1951.*

People have no idea how our system of government works. . . . We, I think, are equally ignorant of their system.

—*Robert F. Kennedy. Journal entry during his trip to the Soviet Union, 1955.*

All I ask is that before we take any more drastic steps that we receive something from the Soviet Union other than a smile and a promise—a smile that could be as crooked and a promise that could be as empty as they have been in the past. We must have peaceful coexistence with Russia, but if we and our allies are weak, there will be no peace—there will be no coexistence.

—*Robert F. Kennedy. Speech, Georgetown University, October 1955.*

We are still too often doing too little too late to recognize and assist the irresistible movements for independence that are sweeping one dependent territory after another.

—*Robert F. Kennedy. Article,* New York Times Magazine, *April 8, 1956.*

If we are going to win the present conflict with the Soviet Union, we can no longer support the exploitation of native people by Western nations. We supported the French in Indochina far too long.

—*Robert F. Kennedy. Address, Communion breakfast, Fordham University, March 1956.*

Our task is to convince [the Soviet Union and the People's Republic of China] that aggression and subversion will not be profitable routes to pursue [their] ends. Open and peaceful competition—for prestige, for markets, for scientific achievement, even for men's minds—is something else again. For if freedom and communism were to compete for man's allegiance in a world of peace, I would look to the future with ever-increasing confidence.

—*John F. Kennedy. State of the Union Address, January 30, 1961.*

We are in truth the last hope on earth. If we do not stand up now—if we do not stand from among the conflicting ideas of neutralism, resignation, isolation, and indifference—then all will be lost, and one by one free countries of the earth will fall until finally the direct assault will begin on the great citadel—the United States.

—*John F. Kennedy as a U.S.*
Senator, 1954.

What we must offer [South Vietnam] is a revolution—a political and social revolution far superior to anything the communists can offer.

—*John F. Kennedy, to The*
Friends of Vietnam, 1957.

Every time a country, regardless of how far away from our borders . . . passes behind the Iron Curtain, the security of the United States is thereby endangered.

—*John F. Kennedy. Campaign*
speech, 1960.

We must come forward with the answer to how a nation, devoted to freedom and individual rights and respect for the law, can stand effectively against an implacable enemy who plays by different rules and knows only the law of the jungle.

—*Robert F. Kennedy. Speech,*
Law Day Exercises, Georgia
Law School, May 6, 1961.

It is such nonsense to have to waste time prosecuting the Communist Party. It couldn't be more feeble and less of a threat, and besides, its membership consists largely of FBI agents.

—*Robert F. Kennedy. Interview,*
London Sunday Times,
December 1961.

At a press conference in Paris just days before President Kennedy was to meet Soviet Premier Nikita Khrushchev, a reporter asked him what he would think if he were in Khrushchev's place. Kennedy answered with a long, apparently unprepared, statement, only a portion of which is included here, which was remarkable for its diplomacy, yet did not contribute to the "weakness" which the Soviets perceived in Kennedy:

I suppose if I were in Mr. Khrushchev's place, it would be because I was Mr. Khrushchev and had lived his life, and therefore I would look to the West and I would see a good deal of reports of disagreement. . . . I would see distinguished American correspondents with great influence take a different view on what actions the United States should take. I would see Mr. Kennedy under critical attack by many of his fellow countrymen, as well as those who live across the ocean. I would look at my own country, where everything on the surface is serene, where nobody criticizes or opposes, and everyone is united behind me. And therefore, I would draw a conclusion that the tide of history is moving with me. . . .

I hope Mr. Khrushchev is not misled by those signs of democracy which we understand but they do not, but instead recognizes that the United States of America, divided as it may be . . . is united in its determination to fulfill its role that history and its own free choice have brought upon it.

—*John F. Kennedy. Press
luncheon, June 2, 1961.*

I have to show him I can be just as tough as he is.

—*John F. Kennedy. Remark to
an aide before his summit
with Khrushchev, 1961.*

We have wholly different views of right and wrong, of what is an internal affair and what is aggression, and, above all, we have wholly different concepts of where the world is and where it is going.

—*John F. Kennedy. Speech upon
his return from Europe and his
summit with Khrushchev,
Washington, D.C., June 6, 1961.*

One of the ironic things . . . is that Mr. Khrushchev and I occupy approximately the same political positions inside our governments. He would like to prevent a nuclear war but is under severe pressure from his hard-line crowd, which interprets every move in that direction as appeasement. I've got similar problems. . . . The hard-liners in the Soviet Union and the United States feed on one another.

—*John F. Kennedy. Remark to Norman Cousins, spring 1963.*

Today every inhabitant of this planet must contemplate the day when this planet may no longer be habitable. Every man, woman, and child lives under a nuclear sword of Damocles, hanging by the slenderest of threads, capable of being cut at any moment by accident or miscalculation or madness.

—*John F. Kennedy. Address to the United Nations Assembly, New York City, September 1961.*

If you tell everybody that you like me better than Nixon, I'll be ruined at home.

—*John F. Kennedy to Soviet Premier Nikita Khrushchev, Vienna, Austria, June 1961.*

Chairman Khrushchev has compared the United States to a worn-out runner living on its past performance, and stated that the Soviet Union would outproduce the United States by 1970.

Without wishing to trade hyperbole with the chairman, I do suggest that he reminds me of the tiger hunter who has picked a place on the wall to hang the tiger's skin long before he has caught the tiger. This tiger has other ideas. . . . The United States is not such an aged runner, and to paraphrase Mr. Coolidge, "We do choose to run."

—*John F. Kennedy. Press conference, Washington, D.C., June 28, 1961.*

The tyranny of communism is as old as the pharaohs and the pyramids—that the state stands above all men and their individual aspirations. . . . That is what this crisis [the Cuban Missile Crisis] is all about; that is why our ships are on station in the Caribbean and why American soldiers are on duty tonight in West Berlin, South Vietnam, and South Korea. They are there for the same reason the Macabees stood their ground against Antiochus—for human dignity and freedom.

> —Robert F. Kennedy. Speech, American Jewish Congress dinner, where he received the Rabbi Stephen S. Wise Award, October 28, 1962.

A little boy in a Russian elementary school, when asked to describe the United States, said, "The United States is a sad country where workers and peasants are starving under capitalist exploitation by the cynical ruling classes."

"Correct," said the teacher, "and what is the major goal of the Soviet Union?"

"To catch up with the United States."

> —Robert F. Kennedy. Speech, New York, January 22, 1963.

No government or social system is so evil that its people must be considered as lacking in virtue. As Americans, we find communism profoundly repugnant as a negation of personal freedom and dignity. But we can still hail the Russian people for their many achievements—in science and space, in economic and industrial growth, in culture and in acts of courage.

> —John F. Kennedy. Speech, American University, Washington, D.C., June 10, 1963.

Freedom has many flaws and our democracy is imperfect, but we have never had to put up a wall to keep our people in.

> —John F. Kennedy. Speech at City Hall, West Berlin, June 26, 1963.

Communism has never come to power in a country that was not disrupted by war or corruption, or both.

—*John F. Kennedy. Speech to NATO, July 3, 1963.*

After ten days of perhaps the most intensive negotiations undertaken by a United States diplomatic team, a final wording of the Nuclear Test Ban Treaty was agreed on. President Kennedy spoke to the nation from the Oval Office on July 26, 1963:

I speak to you tonight in a spirit of hope. Eighteen years ago the advent of nuclear weapons changed the course of the world. . . . In these years the United States and the Soviet Union have frequently communicated suspicion and warnings to each other, but very rarely hope. . . . Yesterday a shaft of light cut into the darkness. Negotiations were concluded in Moscow on a treaty to ban all nuclear tests in the atmosphere, in outer space, and underwater. For the first time an agreement has been reached on bringing the forces of destruction under international control—a goal first sought in 1946. . . .

Of course, the odds are that we will have a nuclear war with China within ten years. But you can't pay attention to the odds. A great power can't surrender if it wishes to remain a great power.

—*John F. Kennedy. Remark in a dinner conversation, 1962.*

Let us reexamine our attitude toward the Soviet Union. . . . We must deal with the world as it is, not as it might have been if the history of the last eighteen years had been different.

—*John F. Kennedy, in a speech at American University, Washington, D.C., June 10, 1963.*

WEST BERLIN

[West Berlin] is more than a showcase of liberty, a symbol, an island of freedom in a communist sea. It is even more than a link with the free world. . . .

West Berlin is all of that. But above all it has now become— as never before—the great testing place of Western courage and will, a focal point where our solemn commitments stretching back over the years since 1945 and Soviet ambitions now meet in basic confrontation.

> —*John F. Kennedy. Television address on Khrushchev's intentions concerning West Berlin, and the planned NATO response, Washington, D.C., July 25, 1961.*

There are some who say communism is the wave of the future. Let them come to Berlin. There are some who say we can work with the communists. Let them come to Berlin.

All free men, wherever they may live, are citizens of Berlin. And therefore, as a free man, I take pride in the words *Ich bin ein Berliner* ["I am a Berliner"].

> —*John F. Kennedy. Speech, Berlin, West Germany, June 26, 1963.*

CUBA

You are under a serious misapprehension in regard to events in Cuba. . . . I have previously stated, and I repeat now, that the United States intends no military intervention in Cuba.

I believe, Mr. Chairman, that you should recognize that free peoples in all parts of the world do not accept the claim of historical inevitability for the Communist revolution. What your government believes is its own business; what it does in the world is the world's business. The great revolution in the history of man, past, present and future, is the revolution of those determined to be free.

> —*John F. Kennedy. Letter to*
> *Nikita Khrushchev after the*
> *Bay of Pigs invasion,*
> *April 18, 1961.*

In a news conference, after being asked to clarify why he had not openly addressed the press on the Bay of Pigs invasion, President Kennedy avoided the issue:

Well, I think, in answer to your question, that we have to make a judgment as to how much we can usefully say that would aid the interest of the United States. . . .

There's an old saying that victory has a hundred fathers, and defeat is an orphan. . . .

But I will say to you that I have said as much as I feel can be usefully said by me in regard to the events of the past few days. . . . [This is] not to conceal responsibility because I'm the responsible officer of the government—and that is quite obvious.

> —*John F. Kennedy. Press*
> *conference, Washington, D.C.,*
> *April 21, 1961.*

[John F. Kennedy Jr.] is still too young to realize what has happened here, but I will make it my business to tell him the story of your courage as he grows up. It is my wish and hope that someday he may be a man at least half as brave as the members of Brigade 2506.

> —*Jacqueline Kennedy,*
> *addressing the veterans of*
> *Brigade 2506, the Cuban-*
> *Americans who fought at the*
> *Bay of Pigs, Miami, Florida,*
> *1962.*

I can assure you that this flag will be returned to the Brigade in a free Havana!

> —John F. Kennedy, upon being presented with the flag of the Cuban-American exile army, Brigade 2506, Miami, Florida, 1962.

I think we would have sent large numbers of troops into Laos if it hadn't been for Cuba.

> —Robert F. Kennedy, commenting on the impact of the Bay of Pigs fiasco, Robert F. Kennedy Oral History, JFK Library.

This urgent transformation of Cuba into an important strategic base—by the presence of these large, long-range, and clearly offensive weapons of sudden mass destruction—constitutes an explicit threat to the peace and security of all the Americas.

Neither the United States of America nor the world community of nations can tolerate deliberate deception and offensive threats on the part of any nation, large or small. We no longer live in a world where only the actual firing of weapons represents a sufficient challenge to a nation's security or constitute maximum peril.

The 1930s taught us a clear lesson: aggressive conduct, if allowed to go unchecked, ultimately leads to war. This nation is opposed to war. We are also true to our word. Our unswerving objective, therefore, must be to prevent the use of these missiles against this or any other country.

> —John F. Kennedy. Television speech, October 22, 1962.

Now I know how Tojo felt when he was planning Pearl Harbor.

> —*Robert F. Kennedy in the early stages of the crisis, when advisers were proposing air strikes. From* Thirteen Days, *by Robert F. Kennedy, 1969.*

I guess this is the week I earn my salary.

> —*John F. Kennedy. Remark during the Cuban Missile Crisis, April 1961.*

Inexplicably I thought of when he was ill and almost died; when he lost his child; when he learned that our oldest brother had been killed.

> —*Robert F. Kennedy, on John F. Kennedy's mood as the missile crisis reached a head. From* Thirteen Days, *1969.*

The record of recent weeks shows real progress and we are hopeful that further progress can be made. The completion of the commitment on both sides and the achievement of a peaceful solution to the Cuban crisis might well open the door to the solution of other outstanding problems.

May I add this final thought in this week of Thanksgiving: There is much for which we can be grateful as we look back to where we stood only four weeks ago—the unity of this hemisphere, the support of our allies, and the calm determination of the American people. These qualities will be tested many more times in this decade, but we have increased reason to be confident that those qualities will continue to serve the cause of freedom with distinction in the years to come.

> —*John F. Kennedy. Statement announcing the withdrawal of missiles from Cuba, news conference, Washington, D.C., November 20, 1962.*

Barbara Tuchman's *The Guns of August* had made a great impression on the President. "I am not going to follow a course which will allow anyone to write a comparable book about this time, *The Missiles of October*," he said to me that Saturday night, October 26. "If anybody is around to write after this, they are going to understand that we made every effort to find peace and every effort to give our adversary room to move. I am not going to push the Russians an inch beyond what is necessary."

> —*Robert F. Kennedy.* Thirteen
> Days, *1969.*

The final lesson of the Cuban missile crisis is the importance of placing ourselves in the other country's shoes.

> —*Robert F. Kennedy.* Thirteen
> Days, *1969.*

If there is a single element in our posture toward Latin America that symbolizes an archaic Cold War strategy, it is the effort to isolate the Republic of Cuba.

> —*Edward M. Kennedy. Address,*
> *Chicago Council on Foreign*
> *Relations, October 12, 1971.*

VIETNAM

Because of the great U.S. war aid to the French, we are being closely identified with the French, the result being that we have also become quite unpopular. Our mistake has been not to insist on definite political reforms by the French toward the natives as prerequisite to any aid. As it stands now, we are becoming more and more involved to a point where we can't back out. It doesn't seem to be a picture with a very bright future.

> —*Robert F. Kennedy. Letter to*
> *his father from Saigon,*
> *October 28, 1951.*

We have allied ourselves to the desperate effort of a French regime to hang on to the remnants of empire. . . . To check the southern drive of communism makes sense, but not only through reliance on the force of arms. The task is rather to build strong native noncommunist sentiment within these areas and rely on that as a spearhead of defense rather than upon the legions of General de Lattre, brilliant though he may be, and to do this apart from and in defiance of innately nationalistic aims spells foredoomed failure.

> —*John F. Kennedy. Radio*
> *speech, November 14, 1951.*

I am frankly of the belief that no amount of American military assistance in Indochina can conquer an enemy which is everywhere, and at the same time nowhere, an enemy of the people which has the sympathy and covert support of the people.

> —*John F. Kennedy. Senate*
> *speech, April 6, 1954.*

The war can never be successful unless large numbers of the people of Vietnam are won over from their sullen neutrality and open hostility to it . . . [and] are assured beyond doubt that complete independence will be theirs at the conclusion of the war.

> —*John F. Kennedy, then a U.S.*
> *senator, June 30, 1953.*

We have a problem in trying to make our power credible, and Vietnam looks like the place.

> —*John F. Kennedy, after his*
> *summit with Soviet Premier*
> *Nikita Khrushchev, 1961.*

This is a new kind of war, but war, it is, in a very real sense of the word. It is a war fought not by massive divisions but secretly by terror, assassination, ambush, and infiltration. . . . I think the United States will do what is necessary to help a country that is trying to repel aggression with its own blood, tears, and sweat.

—*Robert F. Kennedy, Saigon, 1962.*

Moving beyond the traditional roles of our military forces, we have achieved an increase of nearly 600 percent in our special forces—those forces that are prepared to work with our allies and friends against the guerrillas, saboteurs, insurgents, and assassins who threaten freedom in a less direct but equally dangerous manner.

—*John F. Kennedy. Undelivered speech, Dallas, Texas, November 22, 1963.*

If we have to fight in Southeast Asia, let's fight in Vietnam. The Vietnamese, at least, are committed and will fight. There are a million refugees from communism in South Vietnam. Vietnam is the place.

—*John F. Kennedy, to Secretary of State Dean Rusk, c. 1962.*

We've got to face the facts that the odds are about a hundred to one that we're going to get our asses thrown out of Vietnam.

—*John F. Kennedy to a friend, 1963.*

What I am concerned about is that Americans will get impatient and say, because they don't like events in Southeast Asia and they don't like the government in Saigon, that we should withdraw. That only makes it easy for the communists. I think we should stay.

—*John F. Kennedy. Television interview, September 9, 1963.*

You have to understand, my husband is a weak man.

> —Jacqueline Kennedy to Daniel
> Ellsberg, who had asked her
> why Kennedy was not able to
> resist pressure to become
> involved in Vietnam.

The United States has made a commitment to help Vietnam. I'm in favor of keeping that commitment and taking whatever steps are necessary.

> —Robert F. Kennedy, 1965.
> Robert F. Kennedy Oral
> History.

I'd be willing to give blood to anybody who needs it.

> —Robert F. Kennedy, in a press
> conference, November 5,
> 1965, on students who were
> criticized for trying to donate
> blood to North Vietnam.
> Robert in turn was attacked
> for his comment.

The last time I spoke out I didn't have any influence on policy, and I was hurt politically. I'm afraid that by speaking out I just make Lyndon do the opposite, out of spite.

> —Robert F. Kennedy, to
> journalist Jack Newfield when
> asked why he didn't speak
> out against President
> Johnson's policies in Vietnam.

Try to raise your mind to hopeful thoughts, try to lift your voice in defense of our nation, and her role in the world, seek to impress a foreign visitor with pledges of compassion and commitment to peace—try to do that and Vietnam, Laos, and

Cambodia will drag you back down to the reality of a war that robs us of the best in us, and makes our voice ring hollow in the world.

> —*Edward M. Kennedy.*
> *Memorial lecture on*
> *international affairs, Johns*
> *Hopkins University, April 13,*
> *1970.*

The Vietnamese war is an event of historic moment, summoning the power and concern of many nations. But it is also the vacant moment of amazed fear as a mother and child watch death by fire fall from the improbable machine sent by a country they barely comprehend. It is the sudden terror of the official or the hamlet militiaman absorbed in the work of his village as he realizes the assassin is taking his life. It is the refugees wandering homeless from villages now obliterated, leaving behind only those who did not live to flee. It is the young men, Vietnamese and American, who in an instant sense the night of death destroying yesterday's promise of family and land and home.

> —*Robert F. Kennedy.* To Seek a
> Newer World, *1967.*

Three presidents have taken action in Vietnam. As one who was involved in those decisions, I can testify that if fault is to be found or responsibility assessed, there is enough to go around for all—including myself.

> —*Robert F. Kennedy. Speech,*
> *March 2, 1967.*

The alternatives to negotiation are so unacceptable that I continue to believe the effort should be made. Ultimately no other solution is possible. Despite the killing and the destruction, we are in no better position now than we were a year ago— and we will not be in any better position a year from now. . . . We should go to negotiations in an effort to reach a peaceful and honorable settlement.

> —*Robert F. Kennedy.* To Seek a
> Newer World, *1967.*

During an informal talk with students at a Roman Catholic women's college in 1967, Robert Kennedy asked for a show of hands from those who would support an increase in bombing.

All of you who put your hands up, what are you doing to a lot of innocent people? Hundreds and thousands of people in Vietnam are being killed on our responsibility. You've got to think of the implications to your own conscience. . . . What makes us think they're going to give up? Would we go away if they started bombing us?

Our national leadership has now officially told us that all of Indochina is a target of American bombs. The president has said that he would place no limitation on the use of American airpower throughout the area.

And so, as new spasms of optimism govern the rhetoric of where we stand in Indochina, our military planners glibly talk of "saturation bombing" and "close air support" and "protective reaction" and other strategies and labels, all devoid of moral restraint and responsibility—devoid of any apparent concern for the plight of civilians who are bearing the brunt of this senseless war.

> —*Edward M. Kennedy.*
> *Statement to Judiciary*
> *Committee on Refugees,*
> *April 1, 1971.*

Vietnam is the most painful lesson we have ever learned about the aspiration of other peoples, and about events which are neither in our interest nor in our ability to control. Our involvement in the war was a mistake, a lengthy, costly, deadly, tragic mistake that blighted our own nation for more years than any other conflict since the Civil War. There was never a light at the end of the tunnel. There was only a long tunnel, made longer by our presence.

> —*Edward M. Kennedy. Speech,*
> *May 1, 1975.*

Foreign Affairs

You can't expect me to develop into a statesman overnight. Right now the average American isn't as interested in foreign affairs as he is in how he's going to eat and whether his insurance is good. Some, maybe, even are more interested in how Casey Stengel's Boston Bees [Braves] are going to do next season.

> —*Joseph P. Kennedy. News conference with the English press upon taking up his post as ambassador, 1938.*

The fires of nationalism so long dormant have been rekindled and are now ablaze.

> —*John F. Kennedy. Radio address, 1951.*

Let every nation know, whether it wishes us well or ill, that we shall pay any price, bear any burden, meet any hardship, support any friend, oppose any foe, to assure the survival and the success of liberty. . . .

To those new states whom we welcome to the ranks of the free, we pledge our word that one form of colonial control shall not have passed away merely to be replaced by a far more iron tyranny. We shall not always expect to find them supporting our view. But we shall always hope to find them strongly supporting their own freedom—and to remember that, in the past, those who foolishly sought power by riding the back of the tiger ended up inside.

> —*John F. Kennedy. Inaugural address, January 20, 1961.*

My fellow citizens of the world, ask not what America will do for you, but what together we can do for the freedom of man.

> —*John F. Kennedy. Inaugural address, January 20, 1961.*

No amount of arms and armies can help stabilize those governments which are unable or unwilling to achieve social and economic reform and development. Military pacts cannot help nations whose social injustice and economic chaos invite insurgency and penetration and subversion.

> —*John F. Kennedy.*
> *Supplementary State of the*
> *Union Message to Congress,*
> *May 25, 1961.*

Nations, like men, often march to the beat of different drummers, and the precise solutions of the United States can neither be dictated nor transplanted to others.

> —*Robert F. Kennedy. Speech,*
> *Day of Affirmation, University*
> *of Capetown, June 6, 1966.*

It really is true that foreign affairs is the only important issue for a President to handle, isn't it? I mean who gives a shit if the minimum wage is $1.15 or $1.35 in comparison to something like this?

> —*John F. Kennedy, in a meeting*
> *with Republican leaders over*
> *the Bay of Pigs fiasco. Quoted*
> *in Richard M. Nixon,*
> *Memoirs, 1978.*

The country is as strong abroad only as it's strong at home.

> —*John F. Kennedy. Speech, St.*
> *Paul, Minnesota, October 6,*
> *1962.*

If we cannot now end our differences, at least we can help make the world safe for diversity.

> —*John F. Kennedy. Speech on*
> *Soviet-American relations at*
> *American University,*
> *Washington, D.C., June 10,*
> *1963.*

Domestic policy can only defeat us; foreign policy can kill us.

> —*John F. Kennedy. Quoted in
> Arthur M. Schlesinger Jr., The
> Imperial Presidency, 1973.*

The American people do not accept a chessboard view of the world, based only on power politics. Our policy must have a surer foundation, grounded in our basic humanitarian values as a nation.

> —*Edward M. Kennedy, May 27,
> 1976.*

Only an America which practices what it preaches about equal rights and social justice will be respected by those whose choice affects our future. Only an America which has fully educated its citizens is fully capable of tackling the complex problems and perceiving the hidden dangers of the world in which we live. And only an America which is growing and prospering economically can sustain the worldwide defenses of freedom, while demonstrating to all concerned the opportunities of our system and society.

> —*John F. Kennedy. Undelivered
> speech, Dallas, Texas,
> November 22, 1963.*

Far too often, for narrow, tactical reasons, this country has associated itself with tyrannical and unpopular regimes that had no following and no future. Over the past twenty years we have paid dearly because of support given to colonial rulers, cruel dictators, or ruling cliques void of social purpose. By achieving harmony with broadly based governments concerned with their own people, we do more than make our way easier for a year or two. We create for this country the opening to the future that is so essential.

> —*Robert F. Kennedy. Speech,
> 1964.*

It is not always possible to pick our allies, nor to ally ourselves only with governments whose conduct we approve.

—*Robert F. Kennedy.* To Seek a
Newer World, *1967.*

At stake is not simply the leadership of our party or even our country; it is the right to be the moral leadership of the planet.

—*Robert F. Kennedy,
announcing his candidacy for
president, 1968.*

Isolationism

In some quarters, it [the American attitude toward events in Europe] has been interpreted to mean that our country would not fight under any circumstances short of an actual invasion. [This is] a dangerous sort of misunderstanding to be current just now. Others seem to imagine that the United States could never remain neutral in the event a general war should unhappily break out. . . .

My country has decided that it must stand on its own feet.

—*Joseph P. Kennedy. Speech,
Pilgrim's Club Dinner, a
traditional event given to
honor each new American
ambassador, London, March
1938.*

The more I see of things here, the more convinced I am that we must exert all of our intelligence and effort toward keeping clear of any involvement. As long as I hold my present job, I shall never lose sight of this guiding principle.

—*Joseph P. Kennedy. Letter to
Senator William E. Borah,
1938.*

I should like to ask you all if you know of any dispute or controversy existing in the world which is worth the life of your son, or of anyone else's son.

> —*Joseph P. Kennedy. Line stricken from a speech of Kennedy's by Secretary of State Cordell Hull, 1938.*

Joseph Kennedy made known some of his ideas behind his policy of encouraging appeasement in a speech at the Trafalgar Day Dinner of the Navy League in London on October 19, 1938. Knowing how much his notions would shock many, he qualified his remarks by quoting his wife's supposed comments on his speech, which included "If you want to talk about that idea in any useful way, you will find yourself discussing issues which a diplomat should not raise." He raised them nonetheless:

It has long been a theory of mine that it is unproductive for both the democratic and dictator countries to widen the division now existing between them by emphasizing their differences, which are now self-apparent. Instead of hammering away at what are regarded as irreconcilables, they could advantageously bend their energies toward solving their common problems by an attempt to reestablish good relations on a world basis.

It is true that the democratic and dictator countries have important and fundamental divergencies of outlook, which in certain areas go deeper than politics. But there is simply no sense, common or otherwise, in letting these differences grow into unrelenting antagonisms. After all, we have to live together in the same world, whether we like it or not.

Rose commented on this speech in her memoirs, Times to Remember:

In terms of the world of today, and the policies we are following toward China and the Soviet Union, this thought can't seem at all startling. Of course, the idea isn't viable unless those concerned do believe in "live and let live." No one knew then that Hitler was criminally insane.

> —*Rose F. Kennedy.* Times to Remember, *1974.*

You have come to me in one of the most important moments in world history. . . . We are engaged in a fight for time. Anything that keeps Britain at peace is in the interest of the United States.

> —*Joseph P. Kennedy. Remarks to broadcaster H. V. Kaltenborn, August 1939. Nazi Germany had just signed a nonaggression treaty with the Soviet Union.*

When a British reporter asked if he felt isolationism was on the rise in America, Kennedy responded with words that enraged the British press:

If you mean by isolation a desire to keep out of the war, I should say it is definitely stronger. I think it is stronger because the people understand the war less and less as they go along.

> —*Quoted in the* New York Times, *March 8, 1940.*

He stubbornly defended this position by including himself and the rest of humanity:

I have very little idea what it's [the war] really all about, and nobody else seems to have much more.

Churchill, Attlee, and others will want to fight to the death, but there will be other numbers who realize that physical destruction of men and property in England will not be a proper offset to a loss of pride. In addition to that, the English people, while they suspect a terrible situation, really do not realize how bad it is. When they do, I don't know which group they will follow—the do or die, or the group that want a settlement.

*—Joseph P. Kennedy. Telegram
to Roosevelt as France fell to
the German Army, May 16,
1940.*

While his father was in London doing all he could to keep the United States out of the war, John F. Kennedy was at Harvard, seemingly immune to the growing antifacist views of his classmates, and still under his father's isolationist spell.

Everyone here is still ready to fight to the last Englishman, but most people have a fatalist attitude about America getting in before it is over—which is quite dangerous.

*—John F. Kennedy. Letter to
Joseph Kennedy, 1940.*

Joseph Kennedy meanwhile defended himself against the attacks of the British press:

I told them they could expect zero help. We had none to offer and I knew we could not give it, and, in the way of any material, we could not spare it. I could have easily said the usual blah and poppycock, but what's the bloody good of being so foolish as that? An ambassador's duty is to be frank, not to mislead. I considered that my duty and I discharged it. What the hell are you worth if you just mislead them?

*—Remarks to a reporter,
June 11, 1940.*

However, he felt the pressures that were drawing the United States toward Europe, and at the same time that the United States was Europe's only hope.

Churchill said quite definitely to me he expects the United States will be in right after the election; that when the people of the United States see the towns and cities of England, after which so many American cities and towns have been named, bombed and destroyed, they will line up and want war.

—*Joseph P. Kennedy. Dispatch to Roosevelt, June 12, 1940.*

I cannot impress upon you strongly enough my complete lack of confidence in the entire conduct of this war. I was delighted to see that the President said he was not going to enter the war, because to enter this war, imagining for a minute that the English have anything to offer in the line of leadership or productive capacity in industry that could be of the slightest value to us, would be a complete misapprehension. . . . It breaks my heart to draw these conclusions about a people that I sincerely hoped might be victorious, but I cannot get myself to the point where I believe they can be of any assistance to the cause in which they are involved.

—*Joseph P. Kennedy. Dispatch to Roosevelt, September 27, 1940.*

On November 9, 1940, back in the States, Kennedy gave an interview to reporters from the Boston Globe *and* St. Louis Post-Dispatch. *His remarks, which appeared in an abbreviated form in the final article, as well as in most books and articles following, caused an uproar back in London, and was the final blow to his ambassadorship.*

KENNEDY: People call me a pessimist. I say, "What is there to be gay about? Democracy is all done."

REPORTER: You mean in England or this country too?

KENNEDY: Well, I don't know. If we get into war it will be in this country, too. A bureaucracy would take over right off. Everything we hold dear will be gone. They tell me that after 1918 we got it all back again. But this is different. There's a different pattern in the world.

Later in the interview, Kennedy elaborated:

Democracy is finished in England. It may be here. Because it comes to a question of feeding people. It's all an economic problem.

And on his role in the situation:

I'm willing to spend all I've got left to keep us out of the war. . . . I say we aren't going in. Only over my dead body.

> *The story ran in the* Boston Globe *on November 10, 1940. Kennedy announced on December 1 that he had offered his resignation for unrelated reasons three days before the interview took place.*

Freed from his responsibilities as ambassador, he took his views on the road:

We cannot, my fellow Americans, divert the tides of the mighty revolution now sweeping Asia and Europe. They were not of our making and they will not be subject to our control, no matter how courageously or exhaustingly we strive to subject them.

> —*Joseph P. Kennedy. Speech, Oglethorpe University, May 1941.*

Despite all his work against American involvement, Joseph Kennedy turned around after the attack on Pearl Harbor:

In this time of great crisis all Americans are with you. Name the battle post. I'm yours to command.

> —*Joseph P. Kennedy. Telegram to President Roosevelt after the attack on Pearl Harbor, December 1941.*

But after the war, when the enemy became communism, his isolationism resurfaced. His son, as president, proved part of this particular statement wrong during the crisis over Berlin in 1961.

Today it is idle to talk of being able to hold the line of the Elbe or the line of the Rhine. . . . What have we gained by staying in Berlin? Everyone knows we can be pushed out the moment the Russians choose to push us out. Isn't it better to get out now and use the resources that otherwise would be sacrificed at a point that counts?

> —*Joseph P. Kennedy. Speech, University of Virginia, 1950.*

We cannot dominate the world. But we can make ourselves too expensive to conquer. This is not a plea for isolation, but it is a plea against imperialism.

> —*Joseph P. Kennedy. Unpublished article, 1948.*

By this time John Kennedy was in the U.S. House of Representatives, and would shortly become a senator. After his informal speech before the Boston Latin School Association, he was asked what he thought of his son's foreign policy views, especially in Korea.

I couldn't possibly have a worse argument with anyone about foreign policy than I have with my son.

—*Joseph P. Kennedy. Quoted in the* New York Times, *November 25, 1952.*

By 1960 Jack was confident enough to claim total independence from his father's views. When asked in an interview about their discussions of foreign policy, he replied:

We never discuss it. There is no use, because we can't agree.

—*John F. Kennedy. Quoted in* Time, *July 11, 1960.*

John F. Kennedy became as much an advocate of American involvement on the world stage as his father had been opposed.

In 1779, before France came into the War of Independence, someone said to Benjamin Franklin, "It is a great spectacle that you are putting on in America." And Benjamin Franklin said, "Yes, but the trouble is, the spectators do not pay."

We are not spectators today. We are all contributing, we are all involved, here in this country, here in this community, here in Western Europe . . . here all around the globe, where it is our responsibility to make a maximum contribution.

—*John F. Kennedy. Statement, press luncheon, Paris, France, June 2, 1961.*

We, in this country, in this generation, are—by destiny rather than by choice—the watchmen on the walls of world freedom. We ask, therefore, that we may be worthy of our power and responsibility, that we may exercise our strength with wisdom and restraint, and that we may achieve in our time and for all time the ancient vision of "peace on earth, goodwill toward men." That must always be our goal, and the righteousness of our cause must always underlie our strength.

For as was written long ago: "Except the Lord keep the city, the watchmen waketh but in vain."

—*John F. Kennedy. Undelivered speech, Dallas, Texas, November 22, 1963.*

An American piled high with gold, and clothed in impenetrable armor, yet living among desperate and poor nations in a chaotic world, could neither guarantee its own security nor pursue the dream of a civilization devoted to the fulfillment of man.

—*Robert F. Kennedy. Speech, Columbus Day Dinner, New York City, October 11, 1966.*

What we do in the outside world must be based on a deep moral sense of our purpose as a nation. Without that sense of our enduring heritage—the values on which this nation was founded, the basic compassion and human concerns of our people—there is little we can do both for ourselves and for others. American involvement in the outside world must reflect what is best in our heritage, and what is best in ourselves.

—*Edward M. Kennedy. Speech, June 14, 1976.*

We must recommit ourselves to a spirit of cooperation with other nations, both rich and poor. We learned a generation ago that two broad oceans offer no real military security. Now we are learning that our economy is also not isolated from the harsh winds of change that are sweeping the world. American jobs, American prices, and American incomes are vitally affected by what happens abroad.

—*Edward M. Kennedy. Speech, February 17, 1975.*

The growing interdependence among nations of the globe is a phenomenon as striking today as the interdependence of the tiny colonies that came together on our shores two hundred years ago.

—*Edward M. Kennedy. Speech,*
May 27, 1977.

Isolationism may remain an illusion for some; it is a reality for none.

—*Edward M. Kennedy. Speech,*
June 14, 1976.

FOREIGN AID

Joseph Kennedy not only favored the proposed $3.75 billion in credits to the United Kingdom after the close of World War II, he felt it should be an outright gift.

The United Kingdom fought from 1939 to 1942 to save its own skin. . . . So we owe the British nothing on that basis. But we have already spent about $200 billion in a war we were told would save civilization. And we had better give another $4 billion to that end, even though we can ill afford to do that.

—*Joseph P. Kennedy. Statement*
to the New York Times,
March 4, 1946.

I intend to be as brave as I dare.

—*John F. Kennedy, when asked*
what stance he would take on
international birth control,
1958.

Throughout the world the people of the newly developing nations are struggling for economic and social progress which reflects their deepest desires. Our own freedom, and the future of freedom around the world, depend, in a very real sense, on their ability to build growing and independent nations where men can live in dignity, liberated from the bonds of hunger, ignorance, and poverty.

—John F. Kennedy. Special message to Congress, announcing the foundation of the Peace Corps, March 1, 1961.

The time has now come for us to associate more closely together than ever in the past in a massive and concerted attaché on poverty, injustice, and oppression, which overshadow so much of the globe. When the threat of military aggression was the primary one, our posture was defensive. But when the contest is one of human liberty and economic growth . . . we have the resources [and] . . . we have an opportunity in our time to fulfill our responsibilities.

—John F. Kennedy. Statement, press luncheon, Paris, France, June 2, 1961.

The war against hunger is truly mankind's war of liberation.

—John F. Kennedy. Speech, World Food Congress, June 4, 1963.

Dollar for dollar, in or out of government, there is no better form of investment in our national security than our much-abused foreign aid program. We cannot afford to lose it. We can afford to maintain it. We can surely afford, for example, to do as much for our nineteen needy neighbors of Latin America as the communist bloc is sending to the island of Cuba alone.

—John F. Kennedy. Undelivered speech, Dallas, Texas, November 22, 1963.

A world that is spending $300 billion a year for arms can spend a little more for health. And it may well be that what we do in health will be as important to world peace and cooperation in the long run as what we achieve in arms control, and at a tiny fraction of the cost.

> —*Edward M. Kennedy. Speech, May 6, 1977.*

THE AMERICAS

Geography has made us neighbors. History has made us friends. Economics has made us allies. Those whom God has so joined together, let no man put asunder.

> —*John F. Kennedy. Address to Canadian Parliament, Ottawa, May 17, 1961.*

Let us once again transform the [Western Hemisphere] into a vast crucible of revolutionary ideas and efforts.

> —*John F. Kennedy, announcing the formation of the Alliance for Progress, 1961.*

In the years following World War II . . . we were content to accept, and even support, whatever governments were in power [in Latin America], asking only that they not disturb the surface calm of the hemisphere. We gave medals to dictators, praised backward regimes, and became steadily identified with institutions and men who held their land in poverty and fear.

> —*Robert F. Kennedy.* To Seek a Newer World, *1967.*

We are going to be held responsible for the failures and difficulties of Latin America. In many cases this will be justified. . . . But we are also going to be held accountable for far more than can be fairly laid at our door. This is a fact of life; it is important to understand that given the problems of Latin American educated classes, it can be no other way. So . . . if we are to judge our own actions fairly, Latin American criticisms of the United States should be placed in the proper perspective.

—Robert F. Kennedy. Speech, Sixth Annual West Side Community Conference, Columbia University, New York City, March 12, 1966.

THE THIRD WORLD

The great battleground for the defense and expansion of freedom today is the whole southern half of the globe . . . the lands of the rising peoples. Their revolution is the greatest in human history. They seek an end to injustice, tyranny, and exploitation. More than an end, they seek a beginning.

—John F. Kennedy. Supplementary State of the Union Message to Congress, May 25, 1961.

CHINA

Mao in China is not likely to take his orders too long from Stalin, especially when the only non-Asiatics left upon Asiatic soil to fight are the Russians.

—Joseph P. Kennedy. Speech, University of Virginia, December 1950.

It will make a great difference to our acts and policies if we treat China as a potential danger and a possible opportunity rather than as a certain enemy and a lost cause.

—Robert F. Kennedy. To Seek a Newer World, 1967.

By some cruel paradox, an entire generation of young American and young Chinese have grown to maturity with their countries in a state of suspended war toward one another. Tragically, the world's oldest civilization and the world's most modern civilization, the world's most populous nation and the world's richest and most powerful nation, glare at each other across the abyss of nuclear war. We should proclaim our willingness to adopt a new policy toward China, a policy of peace, not war, a policy that abandons the old slogans, embraces today's reality, and encourages tomorrow's possibility.

> —*Edward M. Kennedy.*
> *Statement to National*
> *Committee on United*
> *States–China Relations, New*
> *York City, March 20, 1969.*

THE MIDDLE EAST

I think the word "hate" sums up the situation in Palestine better than anything I can think of. There will be a bloody war because there must be a bloody war. There is no other alternative.

> —*Robert F. Kennedy. Draft of*
> *an article on Palestine written*
> *for the* Boston Post, *June 6,*
> *1948.*

There must be an unequivocal recognition, on the part of all countries in the Near East, that Israel is a nation, and that she exists. She has a permanent right to exist and grow and prosper. This is no longer open to doubt, and it can never again be open for question.

> —*Robert F. Kennedy. Statement*
> *on Arab-Israeli War, June*
> *1967.*

Time and time again, it has been the people of Israel who have shown the courage, the genius, and the determination to give substance to their dreams. Coming together from their roots in a dozen nations, they have vindicated the faith of their forebears. They are part of the biblical prophecy, the prophecy that "I will bring them out from the peoples, and will gather them out of the countries, and will bring them to their own land."

> —*Edward M. Kennedy. Speech,*
> *January 13, 1975.*

The policy failure in Iran was massive, ranging from our intelligence to our commerce, diplomacy, and strategy. As a result, we lost major opportunities for modernization, moderation, and stability in the region. In vain, despite the lessons of Vietnam, we poured virtually unlimited supplies of arms into Iran, in the hope that bombs and tanks and planes could somehow ensure the flow of oil to American homes and factories.

> —*Edward M. Kennedy. Speech,*
> *April 2, 1979.*

AFRICA

There are those who say that the game is not worth the candle—that African is too primitive to develop, that its peoples are not ready for freedom and self-government. But those who say these things should look to the history of every part and parcel of the human race. It was not the black men of Africa who invented and used poison gas or the atomic bomb, who sent six million men and women and children to the gas ovens, and used their bodies for fertilizer. . . . And it was not the black men of Africa who bombed and obliterated Rotterdam and Shanghai and Dresden and Hiroshima.

> —*Robert F. Kennedy. University*
> *of Witwatersrand,*
> *Johannesburg, South Africa,*
> *June 8, 1966.*

Apartheid concerns everyone directly because it involves the whole future pattern of human relations. Apartheid is in conflict with the accepted principle of equality in rights of all human beings, and therefore it represents a challenge to the conscience of all mankind.

> —*Edward M. Kennedy. Address,*
> *Senate Finance Committee,*
> *June 21, 1971.*

Will America support peoples of Africa who seek only the "unalienable rights" we sought and won ourselves two centuries ago? Or will we continue to follow policies that isolate us from these peoples— policies that place us on the side of minority governments that deny basic human rights, and that invite the involvement of other outside powers?

> —*Edward M. Kennedy. Speech,*
> *March 23, 1976.*

EUROPE

England will expect America to pull her chestnuts out of the fire.

> —*Joseph P. Kennedy. Off-the-*
> *record comments to reporters,*
> *1938.*

We cannot base our foreign policy on the thesis that the United States cannot tolerate the attainment by any nation of a predominant position in Europe. If we do this, we shall either have to fill the vacuum ourselves or fight war after war to prevent some other nation from achieving that paramount position. This, however, is what we are asked to do when we are urged to make defensive and offensive alliances with the sixteen or more nations to whom we contemplate extending aid.

> —*Joseph P. Kennedy. Comments*
> *on the Marshall Plan,*
> *unpublished article, spring*
> *1948.*

Human history has demonstrated too dramatically that terms such as [those at Yalta] only give birth to new conflicts. The god Mars smiled and rubbed his hands.

*—Robert F. Kennedy. "A Critical
Analysis of the Conference at
Yalta, February 4–11, 1945,"
a paper written for University
of Virginia Law School, 1948.*

In recent years, some Americans have become fearful of a new challenge from Europe. They see the European community as potentially hostile to U.S. interests. I do not share that view. A strong, healthy, thriving community is in the interest of nations on both sides of the Atlantic. It is also a precondition of future political and economic stability on the continent.

*—Edward M. Kennedy. Speech,
December 5, 1974.*

Even without the bonds of blood and history, the deepening tragedy of Ulster today would demand that voices of concerned Americans everywhere be raised against the killing and the violence in Northern Ireland, just as we seek an end to brutality and repression everywhere. . . .
Ulster is becoming Britain's Vietnam.

*—Edward M. Kennedy. Senate
address, October 20, 1971.*

Vital U.S. interests would clearly be served by implementing a lasting peace in Bosnia. All of us are familiar with the massacres and atrocities that have characterized this brutal war. . . . Ending the carnage and restoring peace and stability to this part of Europe will prevent the kind of wider war that would inevitably involve the United States—and under far greater risk. Twice in this century Americans have died in battle in massive wars in Europe. . . . The peace, security, and freedom of Europe are still a vital interest of the United States today.

*—Edward M. Kennedy.
Statement at Senate Armed
Services hearing on Bosnia,
November 18, 1995.*

Diplomacy and Negotiation

After all, the issues over which governments make such a fuss are generally small ones or, at least, they start as small issues.

—*Joseph P. Kennedy. Quoted in the* New York Times, *September 3, 1938.*

Joseph Kennedy was often accused of advocating policies of appeasement, especially after his stint as ambassador to Great Britain. At a talk at the University of Virginia during the Korean War, he answered the accusation:

Is it appeasement to withdraw from unwise commitments, to arm yourself to the teeth, and to make clear just exactly how and for what you will fight? If it is wise in our interest not to make commitments that endanger our security, and this is appeasement, then I am for appeasement.

—*Joseph P. Kennedy. Speech, University of Virginia, December 1950.*

One finds too many of our representatives toadying to the shorter aims of other Western nations, with no eagerness to understand the real hopes and desires of the people to whom they are accredited, too often aligning themselves too definitely with the "haves" and regarding the action of the "have nots" as not merely the effort to cure injustice but as something sinister and subversive.

—*John F. Kennedy. Radio address, November 14, 1951.*

Miscalculation and misunderstanding and escalation on one side bring a counter response. No action is taken against a powerful adversary in a vacuum. A government or people will fail to understand this only at their own great peril. For that is how wars begin—wars that no one wants, no one intends, and no one wins.

> —*Robert F. Kennedy.* Thirteen
> Days, *1969.*

After it [the Cuban Missile Crisis] was finished, he [President Kennedy] made no statement attempting to take credit for himself or for the Administration for what had occurred. He instructed all members of the Ex Comm [Executive Committee of the National Council] and government that no interview should be given, no statement made, which would claim any kind of victory. He respected Khrushchev for properly determining what was in his own country's interest and what was in the interest of mankind. If it was a triumph, it was a triumph for the next generation and not for any particular government or people.

> —*Robert F. Kennedy.* Thirteen
> Days, *1969.*

A lot of people tell me that Britain is relying on two things today: one is God and the other is the United States, and recently you don't seem to have been counting too much on the Deity.

> —*Joseph P. Kennedy. Remarks
> to reporters, London, June
> 1939.*

Here [in London] you make good by what you prevent from happening rather than by what you cause to happen.

> —*Joseph P. Kennedy, on his role
> as ambassador to England.
> Speech, Pilgrim's Club, July
> 1939.*

It seems to me that this situation may crystallize to a point where the President can be the savior of the world. The British government as such certainly cannot accept any agreement with Hitler, but there may be a point where the President himself may work out plans for world peace. Now as a fairly practical fellow all my life, I believe that it is entirely conceivable that the President can put himself in a spot where he can save the world.

—*Joseph P. Kennedy, in a communiqué to Secretary of State Cordell Hull, urging negotiations with Hitler, September 11, 1939. Roosevelt called it the "silliest message I have ever received."*

You would be surprised how much anti-American [the English] have become. . . . I feel it strongly against me. . . . If the war gets worse which I am convinced it will . . . I'm sure they will all hate us more.

—*Joseph P. Kennedy, then ambassador to England. Letter to Rose Kennedy, March 14, 1940.*

It is easy enough to say we should do something, but the real difficulty is—what? My sympathies are completely with the Allies, but they must not run away with my judgement of what can happen to the United States. We may have to fight Hitler at some later date over South America, but we had better do it in our own backyard where we will be effective and not weaken ourselves by trying to carry on a fight over here.

—*Joseph P. Kennedy. Letter to Rose Kennedy, April 26, 1940.*

While in London at age six, Edward Kennedy came home from school and asked his parents for permission to punch a classmate:

He's been hitting me every day, and you tell me I can't get into fights because Dad is the ambassador.

The state department is a bowl of jelly.

> —*John F. Kennedy. Quoted in* Newsweek, *October 30, 1989.*

So let us begin anew—remembering on both sides that civility is not a sign of weakness, and sincerity is always subject to proof. Let us never negotiate out of fear, but let us never fear to negotiate.

> —*John F. Kennedy. Inaugural address, January 20, 1961.*

We cannot negotiate with those who say, "What's mine is mine, and what's yours is negotiable."

> —*John F. Kennedy. Speech, July 25, 1961.*

The Soviet Union prepared to test [nuclear weapons] while we were at the table negotiating with them. If they fooled us once, it is their fault; if they fool us twice, it is our fault.

> —*John F. Kennedy. Press conference, November 8, 1961.*

We know enough about broken negotiations, secret preparation, and the [Soviet] advantage gained from a long test series never to offer again an uninspected moratorium.

> —*John F. Kennedy. Press conference, March 2, 1962.*

After his mother had sent Khrushchev photographs for him to sign in 1961, John F. Kennedy wrote his mother:

Dear Mother:
If you are going to contact the heads of state, it might be a good idea to consult me or the State Department first, as your gesture might lead to international complications.
Love,
Jack

She replied:

Dear Jack:
I am so glad you warned me about contacting the heads of state, as I was just about to write to Castro.
Love,
Mother

We invited the King and Queen [of England] to have a cocktail which they declined. . . . . The Queen seemed to feel the same way I do about them. She said they never lifted her, and I always feel when I want to be lifted up they are apt to make me sleepy and when I want to be sleepy they are apt to stimulate me.

—*Rose F. Kennedy. Journal entry, April 23, 1939.*

May 5 and 6
Great argument on whether it is befitting for the President to serve hot dogs at a picnic to the King and Queen.

—*Rose F. Kennedy. Journal entry about plans for king and queen of England's visit to the United States. The president did serve hot dogs.*

Talked to Chinese minister of Brazil, fellow passenger. From my own experience, I know diplomats shy away from women who seek information, because they are afraid of being quoted.

> —*Rose F. Kennedy. Journal entry, on board a cruise ship in the Caribbean, May 17, 1941.*

Jackie speaks fluent French. But I only understand one out of every five words she says—and that word is de Gaulle.

> —*John F. Kennedy. Remark to the wife of the French ambassador.*

So that's what you look like, you old rascal, you.

> —*Eunice Kennedy Shriver. Remark upon meeting Indian Prime Minister Jawaharlal Nehru, November 1961.*

Well, I think the guy's a little unpredictable.

> —*David Kennedy, when asked by one of Qaddafi's staff what he thought of the Libyan leader. They had just met while David was on vacation in Pakistan, 1976.*

History

Once, the more I read of history, the more bitter I got. For a while I thought history was something that bitter old men wrote. But then I realized history made Jack what he was. You must think of him as this little boy, sick so much of the time, reading in bed, reading history, reading the Knights of the Round Table, reading Marlborough. For Jack, history was full of heroes. And if it made him this way—if it made him see the heroes—maybe other little boys will see. Men are such a combination of good and bad. Jack had this hero idea of history, this idealistic view.

> —*Jacqueline Kennedy, in an interview with Theodore White for* Life, *1963.*

Assassins have never changed history.

> —*Robert F. Kennedy. Remark after the death of President Kennedy, 1963.*

The world has no right to his private life with me. I shared all these rooms with him—not with the Book of the Month Club readers—and I don't want them snooping through those rooms now—even the bath tub—with the children—please take these parts out.

> —*Jacqueline Kennedy. Undated letter to Arthur Schlesinger Jr. after reading and marking his manuscript for* A Thousand Days.

It makes you wonder about history, about Lincoln and men like that—just how much can you believe?

> —*John F. Kennedy. Reaction to a litany of rumors about the internal strife of the Kennedy family presented by* Time *reporter Hugh Sidney, interview, June 6, 1960.*

It is from numberless diverse acts of courage and belief that human history is shaped. Each time a man stands up for an ideal, or acts to improve the lot of others, or strikes out against injustice, he sends forth a tiny ripple of hope, and crossing each other from a million different centers of energy and daring, those ripples build a current which can sweep down the mightiest walls of oppression and resistance.

> —*Robert F. Kennedy. Speech,*
> *University of Capetown, South*
> *Africa, June 6, 1966.*

The work of our own hands, matched to reason and principle, will determine destiny.

> —*Robert F. Kennedy. Quoted by*
> *Edward M. Kennedy in the*
> *foreword to* Robert F.
> Kennedy: Promises to Keep,
> *1968.*

A sense of history and ability to learn from the past is of prime importance to any man in a position of leadership today.

> —*Jacqueline Kennedy. Remarks*
> *on John F. Kennedy's* Profiles
> in Courage, *1955.*

Few will have the greatness to bend history itself. But each of us can work to change a small portion of events, and in the total of all those acts will be written the history of this generation.

> —*Robert F. Kennedy. Quoted in*
> Conservative Digest,
> *November 1987.*

My brother believed that each of us can work to change a small portion of events, and in the total of all those acts will be written the history of this generation.

> —*Robert F. Kennedy, in a*
> *lecture to white South African*
> *students, Johannesburg,*
> *1965.*

It is the duty of our generation to search backward for the footsteps left by great men . . . not to uncover their sins but rather to find the source of their greatness. . . . We must find out where we lost the trail. . . . Only then can we face the task, as my father was fond of quoting Aeschylus, "to tame the savageness of man and make gentle the life of the world."

> —*Robert F. Kennedy Jr. In response to the questioning of John and Robert Kennedy's handling of foreign affairs. Quoted in the* Saturday Evening Post, *April 1976.*

The cruelties and obstacles of this swiftly changing planet will not yield to obsolete dogmas and outworn slogans. It cannot be moved by those who cling to a present that is already dying, who prefer the illusion of security to the excitement and danger that come with even the most peaceful progress. It is a revolutionary time we live in; and this generation, at home and around the world, has had thrust upon it a greater burden of responsibility than any generation that has ever lived.

> —*Robert F. Kennedy.* To Seek a Newer World, *1967.*

John Kennedy referred to the age in which we live—an age when history moves with the tramp of earthquake feet, an age when a handful of men and nations have the power literally to devastate mankind. But he did not speak in despair or with a sense of hopelessness.

> —*Edward M. Kennedy. Speech, Trinity College Historical Society Bicentennial, Dublin, Ireland, March 3, 1970.*

Often, all it takes to turn the tide is one individual, acting alone against the odds. A single voice of courage and understanding can change the flow of events and improve the community in which we live. Sometimes it can alter the course of history.

—Edward M. Kennedy. Speech, June 11, 1976.

I often think of what [Jackie] said about Jack in December after he died: "They made him a legend when he would have preferred to be a man." Jackie would have preferred just to be herself, but the world insisted that she be a legend too.

—Edward M. Kennedy. Remarks to reporters after the funeral of Jacqueline Kennedy Onassis, May 23, 1994.

·6·

Wisdom, Wit, and Way of Life

Don't get mad, get even.

> *—Joseph P. Kennedy. Quoted in
> Benjamin C. Bradlee,*
> Conversations with Kennedy,
> *1975.*

Forgive your enemies, but never forget their names.

> *—John F. Kennedy. Attributed.*

The great enemy of truth is very often not the lie—deliberate, contrived, and dishonest—but the myth, persistent, persuasive, and realistic.

> *—John F. Kennedy. Quoted in
> the* Washington Post,
> *August 19, 1990.*

Joseph Kennedy testified in 1941 before the Ways and Means Committee hearings over the Lend-Lease act. While he was a vocal critic of the bill "in its present form," he stumbled when asked to offer improvements. Mrs. Edith N. Rogers of Massachusetts asked if he could prepare an alternate bill, which led to this exchange:

KENNEDY: I am not an expert on that at all. I have no experience drafting bills. I am afraid I am one of those critics that only becomes constructive after he sees what the other fellow has done.

ROGERS (persisting):   You are a lawyer?

KENNEDY: No, I am not.

ROGERS (now flustered):   But you've had a great deal of experience with lawyers?

KENNEDY: Who has not?

The point is that you've got to live every day like it's your last day on earth. That's what I'm doing.

> —*John F. Kennedy, to friend George Smathers, shortly after the death of his sister Kathleen.*

We must use time as a tool, not as a couch.

> —*John F. Kennedy. Quoted in the* Observer, *London, December 10, 1961.*

Our growing softness, our increasing lack of physical fitness, is a menace to our security.

> —*John F. Kennedy. The Soft America, 1960. Reprinted in* Sport and Society: an Anthology, *edited by John T. Talamini and Charles H. Page, 1973.*

Conformity is the jailer of freedom and the enemy of growth.

> —*John F. Kennedy. Address to the UN General Assembly, September 25, 1961.*

Some men see things that are, and ask, "why?" I see things that never were, and ask, "why not?"

> —*Robert F. Kennedy. Quoted in Edward M. Kennedy's eulogy to Robert, June 8, 1968.*

I do not think it altogether inappropriate to introduce myself to this audience. I am the man who accompanied Jacqueline Kennedy to Paris, and I have enjoyed it.

> —*John F. Kennedy. Speech at SHAPE Headquarters, Paris, France, June 2, 1961.*

I never know when I press these whether I am going to blow up Massachusetts or start the project.

> —*John F. Kennedy. Speech,*
> *September 1963, at airport in*
> *Salt Lake City, Utah, where*
> *he pulled the switch to*
> *activate generators at the*
> *Green River in the Colorado*
> *River basin, 150 miles*
> *distant.*

When written in Chinese, the word "crisis" is composed of two characters. One represents danger and the other represents opportunity.

> —*John F. Kennedy. Speech,*
> *Indianapolis, Indiana,*
> *April 12, 1959.*

No man can see to the end of time.

> —*John F. Kennedy.*

Our problems are man-made—therefore, they can be solved by man. And man can be as big as he wants. No problem of human destiny is beyond human beings. Man's reason and spirit have often solved the seemingly unsolvable—and we believe they can do it again.

> —*John F. Kennedy. Speech,*
> *American University,*
> *Washington, D.C., June 10,*
> *1963.*

Except for war, there is nothing in American life—nothing—which trains a boy better for life than football.

> —*Robert F. Kennedy.*

Engraved on a plaque above Joseph P. Kennedy's desk:

I shall pass through this world but once. Any kindness I can do, or goodness show, let me do it now—for I shall not pass this way again.

The *acting* governor of California.
> —*Robert F. Kennedy.*
> *Introducing Ronald Reagan to*
> *the Gridiron Club, 1967.*

President is in Asia. Vice president is in Midwest. You are in Michigan. Have seized control, Teddy.
> —*Telegram, read by Robert F.*
> *Kennedy.*

I was sick last year, and my friends in the Senate sent me a get-well card. The vote was 42 to 41.
> —*Robert F. Kennedy. Campaign*
> *speech, 1968.*

I have waited a long time for this visit to the Pacific Northwest. Mr. Justice Douglas has often assured me that it is the most beautiful and exciting part of the United States; and as a mere attorney general, who am I to argue with the Supreme Court?
> —*Robert F. Kennedy. Speech,*
> *Seattle World's Fair,*
> *August 7, 1962.*

I have been through a lot and I have suffered a great deal. But I have had lots of happy moments as well. I have come to the conclusion that we must not expect too much from life. We must give to life at least as much as we receive from it. Every moment one lives is different from the other. The good, the bad, hardship, the joy, the tragedy, love, and happiness are all interwoven into one single indescribably whole that is called LIFE. You cannot separate the good from the bad. And perhaps there is no need to do so either.

—*Jacqueline Bouvier Kennedy Onassis.*

John F. Kennedy on the devotion of his secretary, Evelyn Lincoln:

If I had said to her, "Mrs. Lincoln, I have just cut off Jackie's head. Would you please send over a box?" she would have replied, "That's wonderful, Mr. President, I'll send it right away. Did you get your nap?"

Speaking before the American Newspaper Publishers Association, John F. Kennedy assured them he was not concerned about reporters following around the First Family:

Nor, finally, are these remarks intended to examine the proper degree of privacy which the press should allow to any president and his family. If in the last few months your White House reporters and photographers have been attending church services with regularity, that has surely done them no harm.

And on their being excluded from the golf course while he was playing:

It is true that my predecessor did not object as I do to pictures of one's golfing skill in action. But neither on the other hand did he ever bean a Secret Service man.

When Life *called Bobby "the number two man in town" when he was attorney general, Jack said to him:*

That means there's only one way for you to go, and it ain't up!

—*John F. Kennedy.*

The Catskills were immortalized by Washington Irving. He wrote of a man who fell asleep and awoke in another era. The only other area that can boast of such a man is Phoenix, Arizona. . . . Barry Goldwater wants to give control of nuclear weapons to commanders in the field. Now, that's my idea of high adventure. General Eisenhower says that he could *live* with a Goldwater administration. Well, I suppose he'd have as good a chance as anyone else.

—*Robert F. Kennedy. Senate campaign speech savaging the Republican presidential nominee, Catskills, New York, 1964.*

Bibliography

Adler, Bill, ed. *The Robert F. Kennedy Wit.* New York: Berkley Medallion Books, 1968.

Adler, Bill, ed. *The Uncommon Wisdom of Jacqueline Kennedy Onassis.* New York: Citadel Press, 1994.

American Heritage Dictionary, third edition. New York: Houghton Mifflin, 1993.

Andersen, Christopher. *Jack and Jackie: Portrait of an American Marriage.* New York: William Morrow and Company, Inc., 1996.

Andrews, Robert, ed. *The Columbia Dictionary of Quotations.* Microsoft Reference CD-ROM edition. New York: Columbia University Press, 1993.

Apple, R. W. "Death of a First Lady: The Overview." *New York Times,* 24 May 1994, A1.

Associated Press. "Jackie Kennedy: Seeking Privacy; in '63 Interview, She Also Wanted Memorials for JFK." *Chicago Tribune,* 28 May 1995, 10C.

Associated Press. "Joseph Kennedy Announces He Will Seek House Seat O'Neill Is Vacating." *Los Angeles Times,* 5 December 1985, part 1, 25.

Bly, Nellie. *The Kennedy Men: Three Generations of Sex, Scandal, and Secrets.* New York: Kensington Books, 1996.

Butterfield, Fox. "Joseph Kennedy Wins in Primary for Seat His Uncle Once Occupied." *New York Times,* 17 September 1986, A1.

Cassini, Oleg. *A Thousand Days of Magic: Dressing Jacqueline Kennedy for the White House.* New York: Rizzoli, 1995.

Chase, Harold W., and Allen H. Lerman, eds. *Kennedy and the Press: The News Conferences.* New York: Thomas Crowell Company, 1965.

Cleveland Plain Dealer Editorial. "Jacqueline Kennedy Onassis." *Cleveland Plain Dealer,* 22 May 1994, 2C.

Collier, Peter, and David Horowitz. *The Kennedys: An American Drama.* New York: Warner Books, 1984.

Collins, Thomas P., and Louis M. Savary, eds. *A People of Compassion: The Concerns of Edward Kennedy.* New York: Regina Press, 1972.

Commanger, Henry Steele, ed. *Our Day and Generation: The Words of Edward M. Kennedy.* New York: Simon & Schuster, 1979.

David, Lester. *Jacqueline Kennedy Onassis: A Portrait of Her Private Years.* New York: Birch Lane Press, 1994.

Eigen, Lewis D., and Jonathan P. Siegel, eds. *Macmillan Dictionary of Political Quotations.* New York: Macmillian Publishing Company, 1993.

Gaines, Judith. "Senators Son Had Drug Fling."*Boston Globe,* 10 December 1991, Metro/Region 21.

Gibson, Barbara. *The Kennedys: The Third Generation.* New York: Thunder's Mouth, 1993.

Guthman, Edwin O., and C. Richard Allen, eds. *RFK: Collected Speeches.* New York: Viking, 1993.

Hall, Sue G., ed. *Bobby Kennedy Off-Guard.* New York: Grosset & Dunlap, 1968.

Harrison, Maureen, and Steve Gilbert, eds. *John F. Kennedy in His Own Words.* New York: Barnes & Noble, 1993.

Heymann, C. David. *A Woman Named Jackie,* "complete and updated" edition. New York: Birch Lane Press, 1994.

Hopkins, Thomas, ed. *Rights for Americans: The Speeches of Robert F. Kennedy.* Indianapolis: Bobs-Merrill Company, Inc., 1964.

Information Access Company. "Novello's Recommendations 'Disappointing,' Says Kennedy." *Alcoholism & Drug Abuse Week,* 6 November 1991, 2.

Kelly, Kitty. *Jackie Oh!* New York: Ballantine, 1978.

Kennedy, Edward M. *Statements and Speeches of Senator Edward M. Kennedy.* Washington, D.C.: Office of Senator Edward M. Kennedy, 1996. FTP site.

Kennedy, John F. *A Nation of Immigrants,* "revised and enlarged" edition. New York: Harper & Row, 1964.

Kennedy, John F. Jr. "Editor's Letter." *George,* September 1996, 14.

Kennedy, Patrick J. News release, 22 March 1996.

Kennedy, Robert F. *The Enemy Within.* New York: Popular Library, 1960.

Kennedy, Robert F. *To Seek a Newer World.* New York: Doubleday & Company, 1967.

Kennedy, Rose Fitzgerald. *Times to Remember.* New York: Doubleday, 1974.

Knapp, Joe. Usenet newsgroup posting, 1996.

Latham, Caroline, and Jeannie Sakol. *The Kennedy Encyclopedia.* New York: New American Library, 1989.

Leamer, Laurence. *The Kennedy Women.* New York: Ballantine, 1994.

Leigh, Wendy. "Caroline's Precious Legacy." *McCall's,* September 1994, 114.

Leigh, Wendy. *Prince Charming: The John F. Kennedy, Jr. Story.* New York: Dutton, 1993.

Masters, Kim. "Patrick Kennedy's Politics of Fame." *Washington Post,* 7 June 1994, B1.

McGrory, Brian. "The Political Education of Joe Kennedy." *Boston Globe Magazine,* 23 May 1993, 12.

Noonan, Peggy. "America's First Lady." *Time,* 30 May 1994, 22.

Petkanas, Christopher. "Dearest Sister . . . Love Jackie." *Chicago Tribune,* 7 January 1996, N1.

Ross, Elizabeth. "Another Kennedy, Patrick, Climbs Political Ladder—in Rhode Island." *Christian Science Monitor,* 29 August 1994, US/National 8.

Schlesinger, Arthur M. Jr. *Robert Kennedy and His Times.* New York: Ballantine Books, 1978.

Schlesinger, Arthur M. Jr. *A Thousand Days: John F. Kennedy in the White House,* first Fawcett Premier edition, 1971 edition. New York: Fawcett Premier, 1965.

Sorensen, Theodore C., ed. *Let the Word Go Forth: The Speeches, Statements, and Writings of John F. Kennedy.* New York: Laurel/Dell Publishing, 1988.

Sotheby's. *The Estate of Jacqueline Kennedy Onassis.* New York: Sotheby's, 1996.

Tousignant, Marylou, and Malcolm Gladwell. "A Day of Farewells to a First Lady." *Washington Post,* 24 May 1994, A1.

U.S. News & World Report. "Joseph Kennedy II and Kathleen Kennedy Townsend; a Hat in the Ring, a Toe in the Water." *U.S. News & World Report,* 16 December 1985, 9.

Whalen, Richard J. *The Founding Father: The Story of Joseph Kennedy*. Washington, D.C.: Regnery Gateway, 1964, 1993.

Wortman, Arthur, and Richard Rhodes, eds. *Robert F. Kennedy: Promises to Keep*. Kansas City: Hallmark Editions, 1969.

BILL ADLER is the author of over one hundred books, including *The Kennedy Wit, The Cosby Wit: His Life and Humor,* and *Who Killed the Robbins Family?* A well-known literary agent and book packager, he lives in New York.